NASSAU
& The Best of The
BAHAMAS
ALIVE!

NASSAU
& The Best of The
BAHAMAS
ALIVE!

Paris Permenter & John Bigley

HUNTER

HUNTER PUBLISHING, INC.
130 Campus Drive, Edison, NJ 08818
☎ 732-225-1900; 800-255-0343; fax 732-417-1744
hunterp@bellsouth.net

Ulysses Travel Publications
4176 Saint-Denis, Montréal, Québec, Canada H2W 2M5
☎ 514-843-9882 ext 2232; fax 514-843-9448

Windsor Books
The Boundary, Wheatley Road, Garsington
Oxford, OX44 9EJ England
☎ 01865-361122; fax 01865-361133

ISBN 1-55650-883-2
© 2000 Paris Permenter & John Bigley

Maps by Kim André © 2000 Hunter Publishing, Inc.

2   3   4

About The Authors

John Bigley and Paris Permenter fell in love with the islands over a dozen years ago and have turned their extensive knowledge of the region into an occupation. As professional travel writers and photographers, the pair contribute travel articlaes and photographs on international travel destinations to many national consumer and trade publications. The husband-and-wife team have also written numerous guidebooks.

Paris and John are the authors of several other Hunter guidebooks: *Cayman Islands Alive!, Jamaica: A Taste of the Island, Adventure Guide to the Cayman Islands, Adventure Guide to the Leeward Islands*, and *Jamaica Alive!* Currently, they are at work on *Adventure Guide to Jamaica, Lovetripper Guide to the Caribbean,* and *St. Kitts, Nevis, Antigua and Barbuda Alive!*

Paris and John are also frequent television and radio talk show guests on the subject of travel. Both are members of the prestigious Society of American Travel Writers (SATW) and the American Society of Journalists and Authors (ASJA).

When they're not on the road, the team resides in the Texas Hill County, near Austin.

More about Paris and John's writing, photography and travels can be found on their website: www.parisandjohn.com.

Hurricane Floyd

The Islands of the Bahamas were hit by Hurricane Floyd in September of 1999. Abaco, Cat Island and Eleuthera received the heaviest damage, although some damage was also reported in San Salvador, Exuma, New Providence and Grand Bahama.

At press time, transportation, communications and a business-as-usual attitude has returned to most destinations in these islands.

Should you reconsider your trip to these islands? Not at all. Reconstruction is underway as we write; hopefully by the time you read this all facilities will be up and running, not just to their old capacities but even newer and better than before. We do suggest that you make some preliminary calls before you head to the islands, however. Call the tourism offices as well as accommodations to learn about their status. We've tried to obtain updates on properties, restaurants and attractions but changes are being made on a daily basis.

A huge response for disaster relief has been launched by neighbors and friends of the Bahamas. If you would like to learn more about donating to the relief efforts, contact: The National Headquarters, The Bahamas Red Cross Society, 24 John F. Kennedy Drive, P.O. Box N-8331, Nassau, Bahamas; ☎ 242/323-7370, fax 242/323-7404; E-mail info@BahamasRedCross.org.

Contents

NASSAU & NEW PROVIDENCE ISLAND

BEYOND NEW PROVIDENCE ISLAND

x ✿ **Contents**

Maps

Introduction

Are you ready for a trip filled with good times, good food and good buys? Then the Bahamas may be just the place for your next getaway.

Just over half an hour by plane from Florida east coastline lies New Providence Island, better known as the home of Nassau, capital of the Bahamas. This island may be just a stone's (or a conch shell's) throw from the US, but it gives visitors a wonderful taste of Caribbean life. The atmosphere is a delightful combination of British and Caribbean.

Technically, the Islands of the Bahamas do not fall within the Caribbean, but you'll find many of the same characteristics – from aquamarine waters to a lively West Indian style – shared in these islands.

With its glitzy casinos, breathtaking beaches and world-class shopping, Nassau serves as the capital of the Bahamian tourist industry, both for fly-in tourists and for those arriving on cruise ships and high-speed boats from Florida. But this action-packed island is not the only destination in the Bahamas. In all, there are more than 700 islands and 2,000 small cays and islets spread over 100,000 square miles.

★ DID YOU KNOW?

Of the 2,700 landforms in the Bahamas, only 20 are populated.

If you're looking for around-the-clock fun such as you've seen in Nassau, you'll find another version of it on Grand Bahama Island in the bustling port city of Freeport/Lucaya. Looking for something a little quieter? Then set your course for one of the smaller islands, such as Bimini or Abaco.

Just east of the Bahamas lie the Turks and Caicos, a group of islands that features many of the same qualities as their Bahamian neighbors, all enjoyed at a relaxed, quiet pace. From the main island of Providenciales (known to travelers as simply "Provo") to the tiny getaway of Salt Cay, you'll find beautiful beaches, excellent snorkeling and scuba diving, and miles of lazy beaches in these isles.

This guidebook takes a look at all these destinations and the very best this area has to offer. Whatever the pace of your vacation – from mild to wild – you'll find it in the Bahamas. Grab your sunscreen and your swimsuit and come along for a journey through the shallow waters that have captivated travelers since the days when Ponce de Leon came here in search of the Fountain of Youth. The Spanish explorer may not have found it, but after a few days in the luxurious resorts of these islands, you just might!

The Attractions

The tough part about a Bahamas vacation isn't finding something to do – it's narrowing down the long list to a manageable number. You'll find activities of all sorts – from golf to gambling, from sportfishing to shopping.

What's the number one attraction of these islands for visitors from the US? Location, location, location. A short flight will take you from Miami to the islands; some people even make it a day trip. Several islands are accessible by boat, either on a cruise (a multi-night cruise that stops in several ports or a one-day trip) or a high-speed jet boat, perfect for travelers who don't like to fly.

Major Cities

And just where are all those travelers heading? The top destination is Nassau, the capital city both of the government and the tourist trade. Here you'll find glitzy casinos with Las Vegas-type revues, gourmet restaurants and duty-free shops with fine merchandise from around the world.

Farther Afield

Beyond the two resort areas of Nassau and Freeport, the pace is slower. If you crave tranquillity, head to the south shore, about a 30-minute ride from downtown Nassau. Here, beneath willowy casuarina trees, beautiful beaches give way to a shallow sea.

The Bahamas draw many repeat vacationers. The secret of these little islands? Here are just a few:

- ◎ Great weather
- ◎ World-class scuba diving
- ◎ Duty-free shopping
- ◎ Accessibility
- ◎ Numerous angling opportunities
- ◎ Luxurious accommodations

- ◎ Fine dining
- ◎ Lavish casinos
- ◎ A familiar atmosphere

★ DID YOU KNOW?

The word Bahamas comes from "baja mar" or "shallow sea," a name give to the island chain by the Spanish over 500 years ago. The seas are shallow because the islands are actually mountain peaks rising from the sea floor.

The Cost

When is High Season?

As with most warm winter destinations, prices are higher during the winter months. They reach their peak during the Christmas holiday and New Year's. At this time, you'll also be competing for airline seats with the many Bahamian expats who return home to celebrate Junkanoo. Spring is also a very busy time on Nassau and Grand Bahama island for spring break. Generally, prices drop in mid-April. During summer months, prices are at their lowest, falling to a real low in August and September, the height of hurricane season. Check with individual properties for exact dates of price breaks, though; there are numerous pricing plans.

The Alive Price Scale

Prices change as quickly as the sand shifts on a beach. In addition, accommodations offer a wide variety of steps in their price scales. Partial ocean view, full ocean view, oceanside, garden view – each has its own price based on the month and the day of the week. For these reasons, it's impossible to give exact prices here.

For accommodations, our price scale is designed to give you a ballpark figure for a typical stay during peak season. We've based these estimates on high season for a standard room for two persons. Prices are given in US dollars (but, hey, in the Bahamas currency conversion is as simple as it gets – one US dollar is always equal to one Bahamian dollar).

◆ **NOTE**

These figures don't take into account additional amenities such as meal plans, dive packages, etc.

Price Scale - Accommodations

Based on a standard room for two in high season. Prices are given in US dollars.

Deluxe . . . . $301+
Expensive . . . . $201-$300
Moderate. . . . . $100-$200
Inexpensive . . . . Under $100

At any hotel, be sure to conserve water. Fresh water is a scarce & precious commodity on the islands.

All our hotel selections take major credit cards, are air conditioned and have private baths, except in the case of the few guest houses where noted.

For dining, we've set up a price scale based on a three-course dinner, including appetizer or soup, entrée, dessert and coffee. Cocktails and wine are extra. Price estimates are per person in US funds.

Price Scale - Dining

Based on a three-course dinner for one person. Prices are given in US dollars.

Expensive. . . . . $40+
Moderate. $25-$40
Inexpensive . . . . Under $25

For attractions, we've indicated which charge admission and which are free.

The Land & Its History

A Brief History

The first residents of these islands were the **Lucayan Indians**. Historians believed these settlers traveled to the region from South America around 9 AD and lived a quiet, peaceful existence until European discovery in 1492.

★ *DID YOU KNOW?*

Historians still debate exactly where Columbus first made land-fall, but one long-held theory is that his introduction to the New World was at the Bahamian is-land of San Salvador.

The Spanish held the islands until 1718 when the British laid claim to this area following a quar-ter-century of upheaval. For years the islands served as a hideout for pirates; later they became a place from which to smuggle Confederate goods in and out of the South during the Civil War.

The Union Jack flew over the Bahamas until July 10, 1973 when the Bahamas became an independent nation. Today the Islands of the Bahamas is an inde-pendent member of the Commonwealth of Nations; the Queen is the constitutional head of state.

Climate

The Bahamas enjoy a Caribbean climate due to the nearby Gulf Stream, a current of warm water that was discovered by Ponce de Leon while searching for the Fountain of Youth. The Gulf Stream certainly bestows a youthful feeling on those lucky enough to take a dip in the warm Bahamian waters.

However, these islands are not technically part of the Caribbean. Look for slightly cooler water tem-peratures during the winter months, but delight-fully warm water year-round.

Planning Your Trip

Keep in mind that this is not one destination but hundreds. Scattered across a vast region, these many islands offer a diverse assortment of destinations.

Where should you go? The decision will depend on many factors:

- ◎ How long can you stay? If this is a quick getaway of just three or four nights, select a destination that's easy to reach, such as Nassau or Freeport.

- ◎ How much seclusion do you want? If it's peace and quiet you're after, move past the main tourist spots in favor of quieter getaways such as Bimini and Eleuthera.

- ◎ What type of hotel do you want? Most all-inclusives are found in Nassau. Small inns are found on most of the inhabited islands.

- ◎ Are you interested in nightlife? If so, then set your sights on Nassau.

- ◎ Do you want to shop? If so, travel to Nassau or Grand Bahama Island.

Types of Accommodations

 Whatever you're looking for in the way of accommodations – high-rise hotel, seaside bungalow, bed-and-breakfast inn, small traditional hotel – you'll find it in the Bahamas.

Just as varied as the type of accommodations is the range of prices. Everything from budget motels with Spartan furnishings to private islands that attract royalty and Hollywood types is available.

This guidebook covers the places in-between, where the everyday vacationers can enjoy safety and comfort. The resorts, hotels and villas featured here offer all levels of activity, too. Some have around-the-clock fun and evening theme parties for their guests. Others point the way for guests to find their own entertainment. Some are full-service properties with everything from beauty salons to jewelry shops to a half-dozen bars and restaurants located right on the property. Others are simple accommodations where guests have the facilities to cook their own meals.

Choosing a Bahamian accommodation is even more important than selecting a hotel at other destinations. You'll find that an island hotel, unlike a property in a downtown US city, for example, becomes your home away from home. This is not just where you spend your nights, but also a good portion of your days, languishing on the beach, lying beneath towering palms, and luxuriating in a warm sea.

All-Inclusive Resorts

All-inclusive means that all activities, meals, drinks, transfers and tips are included in the price.

In other words, you're free to try anything you like without worrying about spending your vacation budget for the next five years. Ever been curious about windsurfing? Take a lesson. Want to learn how to reggae dance? Throw off your shoes and jump in line. Wonder how those brightly colored drinks with the funny umbrellas taste? Belly up to the bar. You're free to try it all.

Some folks don't like all-inclusive because of the concern (not unfounded) that once you've paid for the whole package you'll hesitate to leave the property to sample local restaurants and explore the island.

We love all-inclusive resorts, but we are careful to balance a stay at one with island tours or visits to off-property restaurants. Even with these extra expenditures, we've found most of these resorts are economical choices. Top all-inclusive choices in the Bahamas include several Club Med facilities, Breezes Bahamas (part of Jamaica's SuperClubs chain), Sandals Royal Bahamian Resort and Spa (a member of Jamaica's popular Sandals chain), and many properties that offer an all-inclusive package as an alternative to the meals-only plan. In the Turks and Caicos, all-inclusive resorts include Club Med and Beaches.

Intimate Inns

If you're looking for peace and quiet, small inns offer good getaways and a chance to immerse yourself in more of the local atmosphere.

It's that opportunity to meet local residents, taste island dishes, and retreat from the typical resort experience that brings travelers to the Bahamas' often overlooked small inns.

Several small inns here are part of Island Outpost, a collection of small properties throughout the Caribbean headed up by Chris Blackwell.

"I am really keen on the development and promotion of small inns," says Chris Blackwell, owner and founder of the Island Records label, which brought

Bob Marley to fame. In the Bahamas, Island Outpost properties include Pink Sands and Compass Point.

Just as you would with a B&B in the US, ask plenty of questions before booking a stay in a small inn. These properties may offer limited services and may be more restrictive. If applicable, be sure to ask:

- ⊚ Is smoking permitted indoors?
- ⊚ Are children allowed as guests?
- ⊚ Is breakfast served at one time or as guests wander in?
- ⊚ Are intimate tables available or are meals served family-style?
- ⊚ Are special dietary considerations met?
- ⊚ Is there a minimum stay?
- ⊚ Does a remote location necessitate a rental car?

Small Treasures Program

This program was first introduced in 1997 in Nassau and Paradise Island to acquaint travelers with small properties under 100 rooms. Because of the popularity of the program, it has been expanded to Grand Bahama Island and the Out Islands, spotlighting some of the smaller properties that might otherwise be overlooked. Each of the properties undergoes regular inspection.

Where Should We Go?

OK, you want to visit the Bahamas. Now the tough part: where do you go? The choices are many and the pace varies from bustling Nassau and Freeport to quiet Bimini and tranquil Harbour Island. The selection means that you'll have a full menu of islands from which to choose.

Throughout this book, we highlight what you need to know to plan a trip that suits you, whether you want fine dining, beautiful beaches or top-notch shopping. We'll explain how to reach the island and, once there, how best to get to your hotel. Once you're unpacked, we'll have a look at the best ways to get around – rental cars, scooters, bicycles, taxis and public buses.

The Bahamas boasts a wide variety of sporting activities, both on land and on water. World-class golfing, challenging hikes, tennis with instruction by resident pros, scuba diving, deep-sea fishing and adventurous bicycle trips are found across the island.

Choosing A Resort Area

Here's a rundown of the major destinations:

ABACO ISLANDS
Population: 10,000
Area: 650 square miles

This chain is nicknamed the "Top of the Bahamas" and is a popular destination with sailors. These islands are noted for their New England architecture, a reminder of the founders who came to the region after the American Revolution.

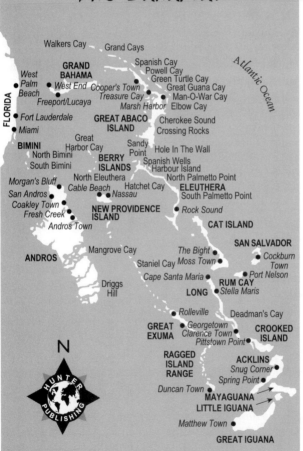

The Islands of The Bahamas

Walkers Cay   Grand Cays

GRAND BAHAMA

Spanish Cay
Powell Cay
Green Turtle Cay

West Palm Beach
● West End   Cooper's Town
Treasure Cay ●   Great Guana Cay
Man-O-War Cay

FLORIDA

Freeport/Lucaya   Marsh Harbor   Elbow Cay

● Fort Lauderdale   **GREAT ABACO ISLAND**   Cherokee Sound

● Miami   Crossing Rocks

Great Harbor Cay

BIMINI
North Bimini   Sandy Point   Hole In The Wall
BERRY ISLANDS   Spanish Wells
South Bimini   Harbour Island

Morgan's Bluff ●   North Eleuthera   North Palmetto Point
San Andros ●   Cable Beach   Hatchet Cay   **ELEUTHERA**
Coakley Town ●   ● Nassau   South Palmetto Point
Fresh Creek ●   **NEW PROVIDENCE ISLAND**   ● Rock Sound
Andros Town   **CAT ISLAND**

ANDROS   Mangrove Cay   The Bight ●   **SAN SALVADOR**
Staniel Cay   Moss Town ●   ● Cockburn Town
Cape Santa Maria ●   ● Port Nelson
Driggs Hill   **RUM CAY**
LONG ● Stella Maris

● Rolleville   Deadman's Cay

GREAT EXUMA ● Georgetown   **CROOKED ISLAND**
Clarence Town ●
Pittstown Point ●

N

RAGGED ISLAND RANGE   **ACKLINS**
Snug Corner ●
Spring Point ●
Duncan Town ●   **MAYAGUANA**
LITTLE IGUANA

Matthew Town ●

GREAT IGUANA

Atlantic Ocean

NOT TO SCALE   © 2000 HUNTER PUBLISHING, INC

ACKLINS AND CROOKED ISLANDS
Population: 412
Area: 92 square miles

These southern islands are divided by a narrow passage. They are little explored, with small villages, remote beaches and good bonefishing.

ANDROS ISLANDS
Population: 8,180
Area: 2,300 square miles

These islands are known for their gamefishing. Andros is the largest Bahamian island and is often called the "Bonefishing Capital of the World." The island is also located on the fringe of the third-largest barrier reef in the world, making it a popular destination for scuba divers.

THE BERRY ISLANDS
Population: 700
Area: 12 square miles

The small Berries are popular with yachties, anglers, and divers.

BIMINI ISLANDS
Population: 1,600
Area: 9 square miles

Best known as just Bimini, these islands are tops with sportsfishermen and are known as the "Big Game Fishing Capital of the Globe." Once the roost of writer Ernest Hemingway, they are still a favorite with sportsmen.

CAT ISLAND
Population: 1,698
Area: 150 square miles

This 50-mile-long island is one of the prettiest in the Bahamas, thanks to its pink sand beaches and rolling hills (including the highest point in the Bahamas).

ELEUTHERA/ HARBOUR ISLAND
Population: 10,600
Area: 200 square miles

Skinny Eleuthera is under three miles wide but packs in a lot of activity. The island is especially known for its pineapples. Harbour Island, a short ferry ride away, is known for its New England architecture and pink sand beaches. Eleuthera is a favorite with yachties and snorkelers, who find good snorkeling just offshore.

THE EXUMAS
Population: 4,000
Area: 112 square miles

This chain consists of 365 cays and islands, making it a popular boating destination.

GRAND BAHAMA ISLAND
Population: 50,000
Area: 530 square miles

The second most visited island in the Bahamas, this island is home to Freeport, the country's second-largest city. Snorkelers, scuba divers, golfers, shoppers and more find plenty of diversions here.

INAGUA
Population: 985
Area: 645 square miles

This island in the far south has a protected flamingo sanctuary and a desert-like climate.

LONG ISLAND
Population: 254
Area: 173 square miles

At 75 miles long, Long Island is known for its beautiful beaches.

NEW PROVIDENCE ISLAND
Population: 171,542
Area: 80 square miles

Home of Nassau and Paradise Island, this is bullseye for the Bahamian tourism industry. Around-the-clock action in the form of casinos and live shows fill evenings, while daytime fun can include everything from golf to scuba diving to duty-free shopping.

SAN SALVADOR AND RUM CAY
Population: 465
Area: 63 square miles

The island where Christopher Columbus first landed in the Bahamas is still remote and quiet, with most residents engaged in farming or fishing.

Bahamas Trivia

- ◎ Which island produces nearly a million pounds of salt a year? (Inagua)

- ◎ Where did Columbus make his first landfall in the New World? (San Salvador)

- ◎ Which Bahama island did Ernest Hemingway often call home? (Bimini)

- ◎ What is the largest landmass in the Bahamas? (Andros)

- ◎ What island is famous for its sweet pineapples? (Eleuthera)

- ◎ What island group is called "The Sailing Capital of the World?" (Abaco)

Nuts & Bolts

Getting There

By Air

Travelers to the Bahamas have numerous choices, thanks to the popularity of these islands and their proximity to the US. Search both scheduled carriers and charter companies for good prices and good connections.

The national carrier of the Bahamas is **Bahamasair**. The airline offers service to 18 destinations in these islands as well as Miami-Nassau, Ft. Lauderdale-Nassau, West Palm Beach-Nassau, and Orlando-Nassau. The carrier also offers service from West Palm Beach to Marsh Harbour and Miami to San Salvador. www.bahamasair.com.

Air Canada, ☎ 800/776-3000, has service from Toronto and Montreal to Nassau. www.aircanada.com.

Air Jamaica, ☎ 800/523-5585, offers service from Montego Bay to Nassau. www.airjamaica.com.

American Eagle, ☎ 800/433-7300. Flights from Miami to Abaco, Eleuthera, Exuma, Grand Bahama Island (Freeport) and Nassau (New Providence Island); Orlando to Nassau. www.aa.com.

Bahamasair, ☎ 800/222-4262, has flights from West Palm Beach to Marsh Harbour; Miami to Eleuthera, Freeport, Nassau, San SaLvador and Exuma; Miami to Nassau; Orlando to Nassau. Domestic flights from Nassau (to Abaco, the Acklins, Andros, Bimini, Cat Island, Crooked Island,

Eletheura, Inagaua, Long Island, Mayaguana) and Grand Bahama Island (to Andros, Bimini, Eleuthera). www.bahamasair.com.

Bimini Island Air, ☎ 954/938-9524, has flights from Miami to South Bimini; from Ft. Lauderdale to South Bimini. No scheduled service, charter only. www.flybia.com.

British Airways, ☎ 800/247-9297, flies from London to Nassau. www.britishairways.com.

Comair, ☎ 800/241-1212, has service from Orlando and Cincinnati to Nassau. www.fly-comair.com.

Continental Connection, ☎ 800/231-0856, has flights from Ft. Lauderdale and Miami to Marsh Harbour, Treasure Cay, Freeport, Nassau and North Eleuthera; from West Palm Beach to Freeport and Nassau. www.gulfstreamair.com.

Delta Air Lines, ☎ 800/241-4141, has service from Atlanta, New York, DFW to Nassau. www.deltaairlines.com.

Island Air Charters, ☎ 305/359-9942. Flights from Ft. Lauderdale to South Bimini. No scheduled service, charter only.

Island Express, ☎ 954/359-0380, has flights from Ft. Lauderdale to Marsh Harbour and Treasure Cay.

Lynx Air, ☎ 800/596-9247, has service from Ft. Lauderdale to Cat Island.

Paradise Islands Airways, ☎ 800/SUN-7202, offers service from Miami, Ft. Lauderdale and West Palm Beach to Nassau.

Twin Air, ☎ 954/359-8266, has flights from Ft Lauderdale to Treasure Cay.

USAirways Express, ☎ 800/428-4322, has flights from West Palm Beach to Marsh Harbour and Treasure Cay; Orlando to Treasure Cay; Fort Lauderdale to Eleuthera; and Charlotte and Philadelphia to Nassau. www.usairways.com.

Walker's International, ☎ 800/925-5377, offers service from Ft. Lauderdale to Walker's Cay.

◆ TIP

Low-cost flights can be obtained through charter companies during high season. Ask your travel agent to check with charter and tour companies offering air-only and air-land packages.

Charter Flights

Charter air service is a popular option both because of the proximity to the US mainland and the closeness of the islands. With charter service, you can set your departure time to meet your schedule. Some island-based charter companies:

Abaco Aviation Centre, Marsh Harbour International Airport, ☎ 242/367-2266, fax 242/367-3256. Service between Abaco and all destinations in the Bahamas and Florida.

Cat Island Air, Nassau International Airport, ☎ 242/377-3318, fax 242/377-3321. Service throughout the Bahamas and the Caribbean; daily flights from Cat Island to Great Harbour Cay, Moore's Island and Sandy Point, Abaco, Rum Cay.

Cleare Air, Nassau International Airport, ☎ 242/377-0341, fax 242/377-3296. Domestic and international charter services.

Congo Air, Nassau, ☎ 242/377-5382 or 377-3362, fax 242/377-7413; in Congo Town (South Andros), ☎ 242/369-2632. Airline of South Andros; twice-daily service to Andros, services to Freeport, Ragged Island, Mangrove Cay and Miami.

Le Air Charter Services Limited, Nassau International Airport, ☎ 242/377-2356 or 377-2357, fax 242/377-3375; www.bahamasnet.com/heair.htmt. Service throughout the Bahamas.

Major's Air Services, Freeport International Airport, ☎ 242/352-5778 or 352-5781, fax 242/352-5788; www.BahamasVG.com/cdk/majorair.html. Regular flights to Treasure Cay, Marsh Harbour, Walkers Cay, Moore's Island, Bimini, San Andros, Fresh Creek, Mangrove Cay, Congo Town, Governors Harbour, North Eleuthera, Long Island, Exuma.

Sandpiper Air and 4 Way Charter, Nassau International Airport, ☎ 242/377-5751, fax 242/377-3143. Service throughout the Bahamas and to Ft. Lauderdale.

Sky Unlimited Limited, Nassau International Airport, ☎ 242/377-8993 or 377-8777, fax 242/377-3107. Service throughout Bahamas; scheduled service to Bimini.

Blackhawk International Airways, Ft. Lauderdale, ☎ 954/983-3606. Service from the Bahamas to Orlando, Miami, Ft. Lauderdale, West Palm Beach and anywhere else in Florida.

Stella Maris Resort Aviation, Stella Maris, Long Island, ☎ 242/338-2051, fax 242/338-2052. Service throughout the Bahamas and Turks and Caicos.

Bahamas Seaplane Service, Nassau, ☎ and fax 242/327-0537. Seaplane service and sightseeing.

By Cruise Ship

The cruise industry brings thousands of vacationers to the Bahamas every year. Many travel from Port Canaveral or Miami and stop in Nassau or Freeport for a day of shopping and beach fun. Some lines, such as Royal Caribbean, make stops at the smaller Berry Islands and CoCo Cay. Princess Cruises makes a stop in Eleuthera.

CRUISE LINES SERVING THE BAHAMAS	
Carnival (www.carnival.com)	☎ 800/327-9501
Celebrity (www.celebrity-cruises.com)	☎ 800/437-3111
Costa (www.costacruises.com)	☎ 800/462-6782
Crystal (www.crystalcruising.com)	☎ 800/5CUNARD
Disney (www.disneycruise.com)	☎ 800/951-3532
Dolphin (www.carnival.com)	☎ 800/222-1003
Holland America (www.hollandamerica.com)	☎ 206/281-0351
Norwegian (www.ncl.com)	☎ 800/327-7030
Premier (www.premiercruises.com)	☎ 800/327-7113
Princess (www.princess.com)	☎ 800/421-0522
Regal (www.regalcruises.com)	☎ 800/270-7245
Royal Caribbean (www.royalcaribbean.com)	☎ 800/327-6700
Royal Olympic (www.royalolympiccruises.com)	☎ 800/872-6400
Seabourn (www.seabourn.com)	☎ 800/929-9595
Silversea (www.silverseaships.com)	☎ 800/722-6655

Many cruises are seasonal. Check with the cruise lines for their current scheduled stops.

Bahamas Introduction

By Smaller Boat

Seajets is offering a special fare of $99 per adult, round-trip.

Another option if you're coming from the east coast of Florida is a new jetfoil service run by **Seajets** (☎ 877/273-2538; www.seajets.com). Boats leave from the Port of Palm Beach at 9 a.m. and 3:30 p.m., and from Grand Bahama at 11:30 a.m. and 6 p.m. One-way passage takes just over 1½ hours. Seajets runs every day of the week except Tuesday.

Inter-Island Travel

By Air

Inter-island travel is easy with flights on Bahamasair connecting most islands. For information, ☎ 800/222-4262. Here's a sampling of typical prices:

```
Nassau-Abaco . . . . . . . . . . . . US $120
Nassau-Harbour Island/Eleuthera . . US $96
Nassau-Andros . . . . . . . . . . . US $84
Nassau-Grand Bahama Island . . . US $128
```

By Boat

Mailboats

A unique way to get around the islands is aboard a mailboat. These working vessels depart from Potter's Cay in Nassau and serve the Out Islands. There are about two dozen mailboats and they make weekly runs.

◆ **NOTE**

Remember that "run" is a figurative term – these are definitely slow boats. You'll have a real chance to kick back and enjoy the island pace.

The fare can't be beat; rates run about $35 for a one-way journey. For more information on mailboat transportation, check with the Dockmaster's office in Nassau, ☎ 242/393-1064, or the Bahamas Tourist Office.

Mailboats are a true taste of the Bahamas.

High-Speed Boats

Another option, especially popular with Florida residents or those vacationing in the Sunshine State, is access via high-speed boat. Several companies offer travel from Miami to the islands.

The Cat (☎ 888/635-9228) travels from Miami to Nassau in three hours on Sunday, Monday, Wednesday and Friday. The trip costs US $139 for adults, $79 for kids 6-12. The 260-foot, 370-passenger catamaran also offers a two-hour trip from Miami to Freeport, Grand Bahama on Tuesday, Thursday and Saturday; this costs US $125 for adults and $75 for kids.

Bahamas Fast Ferries (☎ 242/323-2166) cruise from Nassau to Harbour Island then on to Eleuthera. The trip leaves Nassau at 10 am and returns at 4 pm. You can also opt for an overnight stay. Rates are US $139 for adults and $89 for children; the cost includes lunch, an historic tour, and a beach visit. A transportation-only ticket is also available for $90 round-trip. For more information, check out the website at www.bahamasferries.com.

Getting Ready

When to Visit

The peak (read: most expensive) time to visit is during winter, mid-December through mid-April. This is the busiest time of year, a season when Americans and Canadians are looking for a warm-weather refuge, if only for a few days, and when hotels and condominiums can charge peak prices.

⚠ WARNING

Nassau is a spring break destination for many students. Unless you enjoy a serious party atmosphere, avoid late March and early April. Spring breakers don't hit the Out Islands so these destinations maintain their peaceful atmosphere year-round.

Good forecasting systems keep travelers aware of potential storms days in advance.

You'll find equally pleasant weather conditions in the "shoulder" seasons – fall and spring. Prices are somewhat lower during these months and reservations are easier to obtain. In the fall months, the busiest time is late October when the annual Pirates Week blowout fills hotels with merrymakers.

Summer months are the cheapest times to visit – look for rooms at 40-50% off peak rates. Early summer is especially pleasant. Late summer can bring the threat of hurricanes, but even that's a minor threat.

Entry Requirements & Customs

Documentation

US and Canadian citizens need to show proof of citizenship in the form of a passport or birth certificate with an official photo identification. Visitors must also show a return airline ticket.

All other visitors must show a valid passport.

Visitors can be refused entry if their appearance or behavior do not meet "acceptable" social standards.

Customs

Travelers arriving in the Bahamas may bring 50 cigars, 200 cigarettes or one pound of tobacco, one quart of spirits, and personal effects.

Only canned fruit or canned or frozen meats may be imported.

US Regulations

When departing, be aware that US Customs will allow US $600 worth of merchandise duty-free. A 10% tax is charged on the next $1,000 worth of goods. You can mail home gifts of up to $50 without duty and you may also take back one liter of wine or liquor and five cartons of cigarettes duty-free. The next $1,000 is taxed at a rate of 10%.

◆ TIP

Before your trip, get a copy of the *Know Before You Go* brochure (Publication 512) from the US Customs Service at your airport or by writing the US Customs Service, PO Box 7407, Washington, DC 20044.

Canadian Regulations

If you are a Canadian citizen, you can return home with C$300 in goods duty-free if you have been away from Canada for seven days or longer. This exemption is good once per year. If you've been away more than 48 hours, you can claim an additional exemption of C$100 per calendar quarter. (You can't claim the yearly and the quarterly exemptions within the same quarter.)

UK Regulations

UK citizens can take home no more than 200 cigarettes or 100 cigarillos or 50 cigars (or 250 grams of tobacoo) without duty; two liters of table wine; 50 grams of perfume or 60 cc and 250 cc of toilet water; and other goods up to a total of £145 (including gifts).

What to Pack

We're happy to say that you won't need to pack a steamer trunk for a vacation in the Bahamas. No matter what your planned activities, you'll find that these are casual islands. Unlike some other Caribbean destinations, which recall a more proper British standard of dress especially during high season, the Bahamas adheres to American standards of casual comfort.

Shorts and t-shirts are the uniform. Be sure to bring along at least two swimsuits (the high humidity means that clothing takes extra time to dry) and cover-ups.

Evenings are equally casual. We've worn shorts and sandals to many al fresco meals on these islands. There are some restaurants on Grand Bahama and New Providence where you'll feel more comfortable in long pants, a collared shirt, or a simple dress; we've indicated these in the restaurant listings.

Nightlife is also laid-back, although you'll find plenty of opportunities to bring out that sequined dress or satin bag for an evening in one of Nassau's casinos.

Swimwear is appropriate only for the beach, so you will want a cover-up, no matter how casual, for lunches & excursions.

We do recommend a few items for all visitors:

- ❏ *proof of citizenship*
- ❏ *airline tickets*
- ❏ *snorkel, fins and mask*
- ❏ *sunscreen*
- ❏ *aloe vera gel*
- ❏ *first aid kit*
- ❏ *cameras, flash and film (we recommend an inexpensive underwater camera as well)*
- ❏ *drivers license for car rental*
- ❏ *swimsuit (at least two)*
- ❏ *all prescriptions (in prescription bottles)*
- ❏ *mini-address book*

If you'll be scuba diving, don't forget your "C" card as well as any gear you typically bring along such as a compass, dive tables, dive computer, weight belt, mesh bag, dive boots, logbook and proof of insurance.

Anglers should pack a pair of polarized sunglasses, helpful on the glaring flats for spotting those wily bonefish. Anyone considering a boat excursion should bring along some non-skid shoes as well.

If you forget something, don't worry. Nassau has everything you'll need, albeit at prices somewhat higher than you might find at home. Grand Bahama Island is another good spot to pick up things you need.

If you'll be making one of the Family Islands or the Turks and Caicos your home base, we recommend double-checking your packing list. Remember, these are remote islands with few stores. You'll find the basics but the selection will be slim.

Sources of Information

For general information and brochures, call the **Bahamas Tourist Office** at ☎ 800/4-BAHAMAS, or visit their extensive web site at www.bahamas.com. Check it out for more information on everything from transportation to accommodations to weather.

Gather as much information as you can.

For information on the Bahamas, call ☎ 800/4-BAHAMAS within the United States. From Canada, the toll-free number is ☎ 800/667-3777. For additional information, contact the office nearest you.

Bahamas Introduction

Bahamas Tourist Offices in the US

8600 Bryn Mawr Avenue, Suite 820
Chicago, IL 60631
☎ 773/693-1500

World Trade Center, Suite 116
2050 Stemmons Freeway
P.O. Box 581408
Dallas, TX 75258-1408
☎ 214/742-1886

3450 Wilshire Boulevard, Suite 208
Los Angeles, CA 90010
☎ 213/385-0033

One Turnberry Place
19495 Biscayne Boulevard, Suite 242,
Aventura, FL 33180
☎ 305/932-0051

150 East 52nd Street
28th Floor North
New York, NY 10022
☎ 212/758-2777

Bahamas Tourist Offices In Canada

121 Bloor Street East, Suite 1101
Toronto, Ontario M4W 3M5
☎ 416/968-2999

Island-Specific Offices

For more on specific islands, contact one of these tourism offices:

Bahamas Out Islands Promotion Board
1100 Lee Wagener Blvd., Suite 204,
Fort Lauderdale, FL 33315
☎ 800/688-4752

Grand Bahama Island Tourism Board
One Turnberry Place
19495 Biscayne Blvd., Suite 809
Aventura, FL 33180
☎ 800/448-3386

Nassau/Paradise Island Promotion Board
One Turnberry Place
19495 Biscayne Blvd, Suite 804
Aventura, FL 33180
☎ 800/327-9019

Travelers' Information, A-Z

Banking

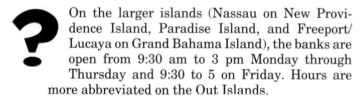

On the larger islands (Nassau on New Providence Island, Paradise Island, and Freeport/Lucaya on Grand Bahama Island), the banks are open from 9:30 am to 3 pm Monday through Thursday and 9:30 to 5 on Friday. Hours are more abbreviated on the Out Islands.

Climate

The Bahamas does not always share in the Caribbean climate enjoyed by its southern neighbors. While the Gulf Stream does keep these islands temperate, they are not part of the Caribbean and can feel the chill of a winter blast of air from time to time. The average high temperature is 80°. Winter temperatures hover in the 70s, dropping to about 60 at night. Summer months show a rise in the mercury with temperatures approaching the high 80s. The rainy season is May through October. Hurricane season extends from June through November. Water temperatures range from about 70° during the winter months to 83° by August. The rainiest month for a visit is June, when you can expect about 8½ inches of rain. July, August, September and October are also rainy, with six or seven inches in most years. The driest months for a visit are February and March.

CLIMATE CHART	
MONTH	HIGH/LOW
January	77/61
February	78/63
March	80/64
April	82/68
May	84/70
June	86/73
July	88/75
August	89/75
September	88/75
October	85/72
November	82/69
December	79/64

Credit Cards

Major credit cards are accepted at most establishments.

Currency

The Bahamian dollar is the legal tender. It is set at an exchange rate on par with the US dollar. You don't need to worry about changing money, however; the US dollar is legal tender throughout the islands.

Crime

Do not leave valuables on the beach when you go for a swim, even if it looks empty.

As in any big cities, crime is a problem in Nassau and, to a lesser degree, in Freeport. Away from these areas, the crime rate is lower but you should still take common sense precautions.

Departure Tax

A departure tax of $15 per person is charged from Nassau/Paradise Island and the Out Islands. The departure tax from Grand Bahama Island is $18 per person. Children under six years are exempt from payment of departure tax with proof of age.

Dress

With its strong British history, the citizens of the Bahamas are modest, conservative people who generally frown upon displays of skin. Most islanders follow a more conservative style of dress than seen in US beach communities.

Bathing suits are appropriate only for swimming; when off the beach grab a cover-up. Bare chests are also frowned upon outside the beach – throw on a t-shirt, guys. However, leisure wear – T-shirts, shorts, sundresses and sandals – will be readily accepted.

Throughout this book, we've included dress code suggestions for all restaurants. In general, expect high season (mid-December through mid-April) to be the dressiest period, the only time when jackets and occasionally ties will be required at a few restaurants for dinner.

Generally, "casually elegant" or "resort casual" is the order of the day, an indication that it's fine to wear polo shirts, khakis and sundresses.

Driving

You may use a valid US or International driver's license for up to three months.

All driving is on the left and British rules apply.

Drugs

Marijuana is illegal throughout the Bahamas. Drug penalties are becoming stiffer, and drug prevention measures more stringent. We also caution vacationers not to return home with any packages that they have not personally packed. We were once approached in the Turks and Caicos airport by a driver who asked us to mail a package for him when we reached Miami. The request may have been legitimate, but the risk is too great.

Electricity

Throughout the islands, electricity is 120 volts AC.

Embassies

The **Canadian Embassy** can be reached at ☎ 242/393-2123.

In the Bahamas, the **American Embassy** is on Queen Street in Nassau; ☎ 242/322-1181 or 328-2206.

If you would like to contact the **Bahamian Embassy** in the US, write to Embassy of the Bahamas, 2220 Massachusetts Avenue, N.W., Washington, DC 20008; ☎ 202/319-2660.

The **British High Commission** can be reached by calling ☎ 242/325-7471; fax 323-3871. The office is located on East Street in Nassau.

Emergency Numbers

Throughout the Bahamas, the following numbers can be called for emergency help:

Emergencies . . . . ☎ 911
Hospital (Nassau). . . . ☎ 322-2861 or 8411
Ambulance . . . . ☎ 322-2221
Med Evac. . . . . ☎ 322-2881
Air Ambulance . . . . ☎ 327-7077
Fire . . . . ☎ 911
Police . . . . ☎ 911

Entry Requirements

US citizens must carry proof of citizenship (passport or certified birth certificate and photo identification).

Visas are not required for stays shorter than eight months.

You will be issued an immigration card when entering the Bahamas. Hold onto it; you will need to present the card upon departure. When departing, you'll clear US Customs and Immigration in Nassau or Freeport, a real time-saver.

Immunizations

No immunizations are required for travel to the Bahamas.

Language

English, with a Bahamian lilt, is spoken throughout the islands.

Marriage

There's no better excuse for a feast than a wedding, and getting married in the Bahamas is a simple task. The regulations are:

⊚ One of the parties must reside in the Bahamas when the marriage application is made (this requirement is easily waived).

Voter registration cards are not accepted as a proof of citizenship.

> ◎ One of the parties must reside in the Bahamas for one day prior to the marriage.
>
> ◎ If either party is divorced, the original final decree or a finalized copy of the divorce must be presented to the Clerk of the Court.
>
> ◎ If either party is widowed, the original or notarized copy of the death certificate must be presented.
>
> ◎ Parties under age 18 must have parental consent; US citizens under 18 must produce a declaration certifying this fact before the US Consul at the American Embassy in Nassau.

No blood test is necessary; the marriage license fee is $40.

You can file directly with the office of the Registrar General in Nassau (weekdays 9:30 to 4:30). When the license is granted, the commissioner's office on the island where the marriage will take place is notified of the upcoming event. If you have questions, contact the Tourism Office or ☎ 888/NUPTIAL.

You'll find that many of the larger hotels have wedding consultants on staff to help simplify the arrangements. Even so, you'll want to begin the process before you arrive in the islands. Contact your hotel, explain that you'd like to come to the Bahamas to get married, and get the ball rolling.

Weddings are free for guests at Breezes.

The Sandals and Breezes properties are especially popular for weddings. Sandals is a couples-only resort; Breezes is part of the SuperClubs chain and is for adults only.

Pets

Pet owners need to obtain an approved permit from the Ministry of Agriculture and Fisheries to bring any animal into the country. You can write to the Director of Agriculture, Attention: Permit Section, PO Box N-3704, Nassau, Bahamas. Include a letter with your full name and address and expected arrival date, final destination in the Bahamas, and information on the pet (species, breed, age, sex, etc.) All pets must be six months or older. The application fee is $10.

Photography

Ask permission before taking photos. In some of the market areas (especially Nassau's Straw Market) you will be expected to make a purchase before taking a photo.

Postage

Air postage for postcards to all destinations is 40¢; air mail letters to all destinations require 50¢ postage.

Air mail to the US, West Indies and Canada is 55¢ per half-ounce. To the UK, Central and South America, Bermuda, the Falkland Islands, the Mediterranean, and Europe, the rate is 60¢ per half-ounce.

You can buy stamps at most pharmacies on Bay Street in Nassau and in the Post Office (at the intersection of Parliament Street and Shirley Street in Nassau).

Public Holidays

National holidays are New Year's Day, Good Friday, Easter, Whit Monday (the last Monday in May), Labour Day (first Monday in June), Independence Day (July 10), Emancipation Day (first Monday in August), Discovery Day (Oct. 12), Christmas Day, and Boxing Day (Dec. 26).

Telephone

Throughout the Bahamas, the area code is 242. Good telephone service is available from The Bahamas.

Credit Card Calls

Credit card holders can dial their companies by calling:

    AT&T Canada. . . . . ☎ 800/389-0004
    Canada Direct (Stentor) . . ☎ 800/463-0501
    MCI . . . . ☎ 800/888-8000
    Sprint Express . . . . ☎ 800/389-2111
    USA Direct . . . . ☎ 800/872-2881
    UK Direct . . . . ☎ 800/389-4444

Access Codes

To direct dial the US or Canada, dial 1 + area code + telephone number.

To direct dial the UK and other countries, dial 011 + country code + area code (without the first zero) + telephone number.

Toll-Free Calls

Many 800 and 888 numbers that are toll-free from the US are also available as free calls from the Bahamas. When dialing, you'll hear a message if the 800 or 888 number is not toll-free.

Cellular Phones

You can bring along your cell phone to use in the islands, but you'll need to register it with the Bahamas Telecommunications Corporation (BATelCo), ☎ 242/394-4000 or fax 242/394-3573. Once you reach the Bahamas, dial ☎ 242/359-7626 and your phone number; from that point you'll be able to receive calls. Roaming rates are $3 per day and 99¢ per minute.

Time Zone

All islands in the Bahamas are on Eastern Standard Time. From April through October the islands change to Eastern Daylight Time.

Tipping

A service charge is usually added to the bill at most restaurants. If not, a 10-15% tip is customary.

Tips are generally not expected for short taxi rides.

◆ **NOTE**

Remember that tips are part of the package at many all-inclusive resorts; check with yours.

Tourism Hotline

Contact the **Bahamas Ministry of Tourism** from 9 a.m. - 5:30 p.m. daily at ☎ 242/377-6833 for hotline help. After 5:30 p.m., ☎ 242/377-6806.

Water

Water is safe to drink, although bottled water will be served on many of the Out Islands.

Weather

Check out the website of the **Bahamas Department of Meteorology** at http://flamingo.bahamas.net.bs/weather.

Websites

For a more detailed list of Bahamian websites, turn to the Appendix, page 287.

For more information on the Islands of the Bahamas, visit **www.bahamas.com.**

For specifics on the Out Islands, go to **www.bahama-out-islands.com.**

While You're There

Formality

The Islands of the Bahamas, especially the more popular destinations such as Nassau, have a very

American atmosphere. You'll instantly feel at home, but should realize that there are some subtle cultural differences.

With its long history of British rule, there is a slightly more formal atmosphere in personal relations. People are often introduced as Mr. or Ms.

Also, as in most of the Caribbean, it's traditional to greet others with "Good morning" or "Good afternoon" and a smile, rather than just launching into your question or request.

Language

English is the primary language in the Bahamas, but you'll notice it is spoken with a Bahamian lilt and follows British, not American, spellings (i.e., colour, travellers, and centre).

Holidays

Expect all government offices and most retail establishments to close on these public holidays:

Jan 1	New Year's Day
Good Friday	Variable
Easter Monday	Variable
Last Monday in May	Whit Monday
First Monday in June	Labour Day
July 10	Independence Day
First Monday in August	Emancipation Day
Oct. 12	Discovery Day
Dec. 25	Christmas Day
Dec. 26	Boxing Day

Festivals

The above may represent all the official government holidays, but by no means is that the end of the partying on this island. You'll find special events throughout the year.

For information on Bahamian festivals, contact the Bahamas Tourism Board at ☎ 800/8BAHAMAS (US), 800/677-5777 (Canada), or 212/758-2777.

☀ January

New Year's Day Junkanoo Parade, Nassau. This is the biggest blowout of the year. The national party celebrates Junkanoo, a day that brings together Carnival and Mardi Gras with brilliant costumes and a fun atmosphere. The air will be filled with the sounds of cowbells and the beating of goatskin drums as well as whistles. Purchase local foods as you watch the parade go by.

Junkanoo History

Junkanoo dates back to the island's slavery days and a time when slaves were given permission after Christmas to celebrate with African traditions. No one quite knows the origin of the term Junkanoo. Some believe it came from John Canoe, an African leader who demanded the right to celebrate even after he was brought to the island as a slave. Other people believe the term came from a French word used for the parade masks. Fortunately, what really matters is fun and everyone agrees on that during Junkanoo.

Starting on Boxing Day (December 26) and continuing until New Year's Day, Junkanoo is filled with parades, partying, and lots of noise.

☼ February

Festival in the Dark. This Nassau event is sponsored by the Ministry of Youth, Sports and Culture and brings together local music such as rake 'n' scrape with limbo dancing, fire dancing, and drumming. Local foods are sold from streetside booths.

Farmer's Cay Festival, Exuma. This event is an annual homecoming for the people of Farmer's Cay, Exuma. You can catch a boat from Nassau to join the excursion. Local foods sold.

Ministry of Health Food Fair, Eleuthera. This unique event was the brainchild of a local doctor who decided to hold the fair as a fundraiser. This international food fair is attended by both locals and vacationers.

☼ March

Heritage Day, Abaco. This Hope Town festival starts with a treasure hunt and includes lunch at Jarrett Park of local specialties including conch fritters.

Pineapple Arts Festival, Eleuthera. The famous pineapples of Eleuthera are showcased at this annual event, along with arts and crafts, basketry, paintings, and plenty of local food. Bring along some money to purchase local pastries, preserves, and other culinary items.

☼ May

Bahamas Heritage Festival, Nassau. Part of the Great Bahamas Seafood Festival, this cultural event features traditional music and foods.

☼ June

Pineapple Festival, Eleuthera. This early June event revolves around the pineapples of Eleuthera, with pineapple recipe contests, pineapple farm tours, crafts, a Junkanoo parade, dances, and a pineathalon that includes a swim, run, and bike ride. For information, contact the Eleuthera Tourist Office, ☎ 242/332-2142; fax 242/332-2480.

☼ July

Regatta Time in Abaco. This annual event, now over two decades in existence, incorporates nine days of boat races, beach picnics, cocktail parties, and more.

Beer Festival, Exuma. Held on the full moon, this celebration honors, well, beer.

☼ August

Staniel Cay Homecoming and Bonefishing Tournament, Exuma. This three-day event pits the anglers against the wrestling bonefish and is scheduled for the first weekend in August. Events include an all-day native food feast.

Emancipation Day, Islands of the Bahamas. Throughout the islands, this public holiday (the first Monday in August) commemorates the emancipation of slavery in 1834. In Nassau, events start with an early morning Junkanoo parade and continue with an afternoon of local foods.

Coca-Cola Bash, Grand Bahama Island. This Emancipation Day event on Grand Bahama Island brings together Bahamian music, local musicians, and plenty of local food.

Fox Hill Day Celebration, Nassau. This event takes place a week after Emancipation Day (because the residents of Fox Hill didn't learn of the proclamation until one week later than the rest of the islands). Events begin with gospel concerts in churches followed by an afternoon of local foods. Held the second Tuesday in August in Freedom Park, Fox Hill.

☼ October

International Month, Nassau. The International Cultural Committee of the Ministry of Foreign Affairs organizes this special event. It includes arts, crafts, parades, and international foods.

North Eleuthera Sailing Regatta, Eleuthera. Locally built boats from throughout the Bahamas take part in this well-attended race. Other events include music, road races, and plenty of local foods.

McClean's Town Conch Cracking Contest, Grand Bahama Island. How many conchs can the conch cracker crack? This fishing village comes to life with plenty of fun on the day of this special event.

Wine and Art Festival, Nassau. This annual event showcases local artists. Enjoy their work while you sample imported wines.

☼ November

Christmas Jollification, Nassau. Shoppers can eye local arts and crafts as well as taste holiday foods at this annual event.

Authentically Bahamian Trade Show, Nassau. The Ministry of Tourism organizes this annual event that showcases locally made goods, including condiments.

Boxing Day Junkanoo Parade, Nassau. Won't be here for the Junkanoo parade on New Year's Day? This parade is an earlier version and takes place on Boxing Day (December 26), a day when the English originally "boxed" Christmas leftovers for servants.

Getting Around

By Taxi

With driving on the left, taxi and limo service are the best way to get around. Rates are set by the government at $2.20 for the first quarter-mile for one or two passengers. Every additional mile is charged at 30¢. Extra passengers pay $3 per person (kids under three are free if accompanied).

On New Providence Island, expect to pay about $15 to get from the airport to Cable Beach, $20 for a ride downtown, or $24 (plus a $2 bridge toll) to reach Paradise Island.

By Bus

Public minibuses called jitneys are an inexpensive mode of transportation and a great way to experience local life. (Although not the best choice if you're in a hurry.) On New Providence Island, jitneys run from downtown near the Hilton British Colonial and from Cable Beach. Jitneys also serve Freeport. Rides start at 75¢ (Have the correct fare because drivers don't give change.)

By Rental Car

If you want to rent a car, you must be 17 years of age and possess a valid US or International drivers license. You may use this license for up to three months.

> ### ✗ WARNING
>
> Remember that the Bahamas use the British system of driving on the left. This can be tricky for newcomers and a real challenge in heavily trafficked areas such as Nassau.

Cost of a rental car varies, but expect to pay somewhere between $45 and $85 per day, depending on model. Major rental car companies can be found in Nassau and Freeport in both the airports and major hotels. Costs are higher on the Out Islands.

Don't assume that a tank of gas is included in the rental price on smaller islands.

Other Options

Motor scooters are also available for rent on some of the islands for those brave enough to head out on two wheels. Helmets are mandatory. Expect to pay about $16-$50 per day (you can also rent for a half-day.)

Bicycles can be found on some islands as well.

Shopping

Shopping in the Bahamas is part of the total experience, especially if you move away from the stores aimed at tourists to enter the world of Bahamian commerce. Leave the resort gift shops (where the markup is fierce) and head to local grocery stores and markets for a true taste of Bahamian life.

Bargaining is also part of the fun at the many craft markets throughout the islands. Many travelers avoid markets fearing high-pressure sales, but we have found them to be delightful places to shop. A friendly "good morning," abstaining from photos until a purchase (no matter how small) is made, and general good manners will go far with the salespeople.

The largest selection of shops is found in **Nassau** and **Freeport**. Shops in Nassau are generally open 9 a.m.-5 p.m. Monday to Saturdays. In Grand Bahama, shops at Lucaya Marketplace and the International Bazaar are open 10 a.m. - 6 p.m. Monday to Saturday.

Following each island section, we'll give you a run down of our favorite shopping spots, from markets to duty-free stores.

Nassau & New Providence Island

Just what is Nassau? A city? An island? Both locals and vacationers tend to use the term "Nassau" to identify the island of New Providence, but the city proper is located on the north side of the island.

Nassau is a compact city filled with activity and history. Here stands the seat of Bahamian government and reminders of British rule.

Island Attractions

For many travelers, the first view they'll see of Nassau is from the cruise dock, located right in the heart of the action. **Rawson Square** is only a few blocks away, and there's no mistaking it. Horse-drawn carriages wait for passengers, who pay for a half-hour ride along picturesque Bay Street.

This area is practically in the shadow of the **Parliament House,** a pink building from which the British once ruled the Bahamas. Until 1972, the Bahamas was a territory of Great Britain. The country still retains many British influences, with the Royal family smiling back from the currency and postage stamps. Driving is on the left side of the road.

For authentic Bahamian souvenirs, head down Bay Street to the frenzied, open-air **Straw Market**. Every imaginable straw good is sold here, and if you don't see it, the nimble-fingered women will make it for you. Expect to haggle over prices here, but overall, prices and goods vary only slightly from booth to booth. Upstairs, wood carvers chip away at logs to produce sculptures of animals, birds, and anything else you might request.

Keep your eyes open for photo opportunities here. Children sell brightly colored coral necklaces, strung by the dozen from their necks and arms. Smaller children knot long strips of plastic, used to sew letters on straw purses and hats. Policemen in spotless white tunics and pith helmets patrol the area. From the quay side of the market, you can watch the cruise ships that dock in Nassau daily. Just steps from the market lie the duty-free stores of Bay Street, showcasing baubles from around the world.

For all of Nassau's ties with history, nearby **Paradise Island** is tied to the future. Here, over the tall, curving bridge that leads to the island, stands the newest and largest resort in the region. Nicknamed the "Monaco of the Bahamas," this is the most luxurious area of New Providence Island.

Once named Hog Island, this area was revitalized by the investment of Donald Trump, Merv Griffin and South African businessman Sol Kerzner, who renovated the Atlantis hotel at the cost of $1 million a day – every day – in a six-month building spree.

The island is also home of **The Cloisters**, the ruins of a 14th-century French monastery that were purchased by William Randolph Hearst in the 1920s and later moved to the island.

Today it has been revitalized by the creation of **Atlantis, Paradise Island**, a mega-resort that offers gaming, family activities, and high dollar shopping.

Tourists also flock to **Cable Beach**, located 10 minutes west of downtown Nassau. This stretch of sand is lined with high-rise hotels and some of the island's hottest nightspots. Shuttles run between these resorts and Nassau several times daily.

Spending Money

American currency is widely accepted in the Bahamas, although you may be given change in either American or Bahamian money, or a mixture of both. The Bahamian dollar is equivalent in value to the US dollar, so there's no exchange rate to remember.

Best Places to Stay

Price Scale - Accommodations

Based on a standard room for two in high season. Prices are given in US dollars.

Deluxe . . . . $300+
Expensive . . . . $200-$300
Moderate. . . . . $100-$200
Inexpensive . . . . Under $100

Resorts & Hotels

ATLANTIS, PARADISE ISLAND
Paradise Island
☎ 242/363-3000, fax 242/363-2493
Reservations: ☎ 800/321-3000
www.sunint.com
Expensive to Deluxe

We looked up through the sea water, the sun filtering down in liquid shafts and illuminating the hundreds of fish around us. Suddenly, the light was blocked by a sinister silhouette – a shark.

Directly overhead, the six-foot predator swam with deliberate slowness, making schools of yellow grunts scurry closer to sheltering rocks.

But, unlike the school of fish and the large spiny lobster on the sandy floor below, we were not worried. Along with other visitors in the 100-foot-long clear tunnel, we merely delighted in the view, surrounded by thousands of tropical fish, sharks, manta rays, and sea turtles in the world's largest open-air aquarium.

The tunnel and the water gardens surrounding it are found at the Atlantis Hotel on Nassau's Paradise Island. The resort is one of several changes that have brought glitz and glamour to what was formerly called "Hog Island." Thanks to investment from outside investors, Paradise Island could now be renamed Fantasy Island – a place where high dollar hotels meet gourmet dining and world-class shopping to create a lavish playground.

The result is an island of luxury hotels where sandy beaches offer daytime fun and casino gambling livens the night, sort of Las Vegas meets the Caribbean. The newest property, the Atlantis, opened following a complete renovation of an existing property.

Cost of the renovations: $1 million a day, every day, for six months.

Sol Kerzner, the developer, is well known for themed resorts in South Africa (including one with a zoo) and his Sun International worked to give visitors to this resort the feeling that they were discovering the lost city of Atlantis.

The marine life theme, or at least symbols of it, starts with dolphin fountains at the entrance and continues with conch shell carpet and even marine-themed slot machines in the casino.

Nowhere is the marine theme more evident than in the **Waterscape,** now bigger and better than ever thanks to the most recent expansion. Here waterfalls splash and churn sea water into fish-filled lagoons that weave among walkways, open-air bars, and bridges. Guests flock to the **Predator Lagoon** for a close-up look at the half-dozen reef sharks that swim a constant pattern alongside barracudas and rays. Above the water's surface, guests watch for the shark's tell-tale fin to break the lagoon's surface; underwater, encased in the clear tunnel, they stand within inches of the sharks. The Predator Lagoon is popular with all ages of visitors, from small children who delight at the diving turtles and crawling spiny lobsters to older visitors and non-swimmers looking for the sensation of scuba diving without getting wet.

Viewing in the tunnel and from the adjacent "sea grottos," visitors hear the sounds of the sea. Lighting in the grottos comes from flickering "whelk" lanterns, creating the mood of an underwater civilization.

The grottoes were created from molds of actual Bahamian sea grottos.

Water activities continue above the surface as well. Near Predator Lagoon, a rope suspension bridge swings and sways over the water. Nearby water tricycles churn across Paradise Lagoon, a saltwater lagoon that opens to the sea where the resort hopes to introduce tropical fish. The protected, calm waters will be used by beginning snorkelers as well as scuba diving classes.

For children, the **Atlantis River Ride** meanders through the Waterscape. Kids hop an inner tube and set off on the quarter-mile journey pushed by a gentle current. Nearby, a waterslide plunges young thrill-seekers into a pool of salt water. Kids also enjoy a children's pool with a sand play area, an **Adventure Water Walk** with computer-controlled geysers and fountains, and **Camp Paradise**, with supervised activities. Adrenalin junkies plunge down the **Leap of Faith slide** on a replica of a Mayan temple. The slide takes an almost vertical 60-foot drop, dropping riders into an acrylic tunnel in a shark-filled lagoon. The temple is also home to the **Serpent slide**, which spins through the interior of the dark temple before emerging into Predator Lagoon.

Along with an elegant hotel, the resort brings to the Bahamas a water park that's unequaled in the Caribbean. The tunnel and water gardens surrounding it are the kind of place travelers either love or hate. Don't expect to find peace and quiet here, or even a Caribbean atmosphere. This is Vegas-goes-to-the-beach, but if you're into non-stop fun it's the place to be on Paradise Island.

All guest rooms and suites are air-conditioned and include mini-bars, in-room safe, satellite TV with in-room movies and video check-out, direct dial phones with voice mail, balconies and king, two double or two queen beds. Cribs, roll-away beds and strollers are available upon request.

Sweet Suite

As you look at the new Royal Towers of the Atlantis, you'll see a closed bridge connecting the two towers. This is the Bridge Suite, one of the most spectacular suites in the world. Perched at a height of 10 stories, this suite has the best view of the Waterscape, all from the comfort of an expansive 800-square-foot balcony or from the living room or king and queen bedrooms.

It comes complete with a dining room, gourmet kitchen, butler and cook, not to mention a bar and piano. Every electronic device conceivable is in place here both in the 2,500-square-foot entertainment area and the bedrooms. We recently attended a cocktail party in the suite and it felt as though we were on top of the world. Not surprisingly, it has attracted some famous guests, including Michael Jackson and Michael Jordan. The price? How about a cool $25,000 a night.

Nassau & New Providence Island

HILTON BRITISH COLONIAL
1 Bay Street, Nassau
☎ 242/322-3301, fax 242/322-2286
Reservations: ☎ 800/445-8667
www.hilton.com
Moderate to Expensive

This historic hotel sits at the head of Bay Street, a reminder of Nassau's early hotel days. It's a warm reminder of our early hotel days as well, the scene of our first visit to the Caribbean. Following a recent renovation, the hotel is now one of the top business properties in the islands, but offers a convenient address for the leisure traveler as well; you're just steps from the duty-free shops of Bay Street here. The 291 guest rooms include satellite TV, desk with modem and power outlet, minibar, voice mail, and more. Business and executive floors are available, and all guests have use of a small beach, full health club, dive shop, and four restaurants.

BREEZES BAHAMAS
Cable Beach
☎ 242/327-6153; fax 242/327-5155
Reservations: ☎ 800/GO-SUPER
www.breezes.com
Moderate to Expensive (All-inclusive)

Breezes offers a fun vacation atmosphere.

This may just be the all-inclusive bargain of the Caribbean. Part of the SuperClubs chain, Breezes is a moderately priced property offering only slightly less than others in the chain. Unlike the sprawling resorts of the SuperClubs chain, the Breezes properties (there are also two Breezes in Jamaica) are somewhat smaller and charge a fee for some premium activities.

Breezes does offer all the amenities of the SuperClubs chain, including excellent meals (one of our tastiest meals in Nassau was a buffet lunch at this property), watersports, bars and nightclubs, and even free weddings.

This 400-room resort emphasizes fun and relaxation. No one under 16 is permitted in this singles and couples resort. Breezes is decorated in bright tropical pastels, from its open-air lobby to the rooms located in the lemon-yellow hotel.

CLUB MED PARADISE ISLAND

Paradise Island
☎ 242/363-2640, fax 242/363-3496
Reservations: ☎ 800/CLUB MED
www.clubmed.com
Moderate to Expensive

This recently renovated property offers double rooms with a queen or two twin beds, as well as a two-story villa called House in the Woods. The villa features a living room with television and stereo, fully-equipped and stocked kitchenette, bedroom with queen bed, wrap around porches, and more.

"No facilities in Nassau or Paradise Island offer the kind of privacy, space, luxury, and pizzazz that Club Med's House in the Woods does," says Kamal Shah, President, Club Med North America.

Nassau & New Providence Island

★ DID YOU KNOW?

The villa was built as a set for the 1978 movie *Le Sauvage* starring Yves Montand and Catherine Deneuve. It was later brought to Paradise Island and renovated.

Three restaurants are located on property and you can enjoy a full menu of activity as well. There's billiards, deep-sea fishing, a fitness center, golf, kayaking, sailing, scuba diving, 18 Har-Tru tennis court and windsurfing. All ages are welcome at this property, although special children's programs are not offered.

Club Med is a great choice on Paradise Island if you want peace & quiet.

COMFORT SUITES
Paradise Island Drive
Paradise Island
☎ 242/363-3680, fax 242/363-2588
Reservations: ☎ 800-228-5150
Moderate

This 150-room hotel is an economical choice on Paradise Island. Rooms include a complimentary continental breakfast daily, and guests have full signing privileges at Atlantis restaurants.

COMPASS POINT
Compass Point Beach
☎ 242/327-4500, fax 242/327-3299
Reservations: ☎ 800/OUTPOST
www.islandoutpost.com
Moderate to Deluxe

You won't find many resorts that list "state-of-the-art recording studio" among their features, but here's one, thanks to owner Chris Blackwell. The creator of Island Records has a string of small, fine hotels in the Caribbean, including Jamaica and Young Island in St. Vincent and the Grenadines.

Located about 25 minutes west of Nassau, Compass Point is away from the casinos and mega-resorts of Cable Beach on a quiet stretch of the island near the upscale Lyford Cay, where stellar residents such as Sean Connery and Mick Jagger have residences in the no-visitors-allowed compound.

◆ **TIP**

You might get lucky and spot a familiar face dockside at Compass Point, as Lyford Cay residents cruise up to the restaurant for a night out.

Compass Point has only 18 rooms, but you can't miss this rainbow property. Look for the festive colors of the Junkanoo festival: vibrant tones of purple, blue, yellow and red. Each individual cottage is decorated in a style that might be described as Caribbean kitsch meets "Gilligan's Island." Guests can choose from five cabana rooms (the only air-conditioned accommodations) or the larger, more private huts and cottages (which include a downstairs open-air kitchen and picnic-table dining room).

Complete your day in the rocking chairs on your private porch that looks out to the sea, then come in to sleep beneath a ceiling fan in a handmade bed covered with a Bahamian batik spread.

After a day on the beach, travelers enjoy a casually elegant meal in the resort restaurant. Californian-Caribbean cuisine is popular both with guests and locals.

Every room at Compass Point is handcrafted and faces the sea. This is a great place to get away from the hubbub of Nassau and Paradise Island.

GRAYCLIFF HOTEL
West Hill Street
☎ 242/322-2796, fax 242/326-6110
www.graycliff.com
Moderate to Deluxe

This historic property is located next to Government House and offers 13 luxurious guest accommodations and spacious pool cottage suites. This building dates back to Nassau's swashbuckling days. The mansion was originally built by Captain John Howard Graysmith, a pirate who commanded the schooner *Graywold* and plundered treasure ships along the Spanish Main. In 1776, the mansion became the headquarters for the American Navy when Nassau was captured by the soldiers. In 1844, Graycliff became Nassau's first inn.

The home has a rich history of celebrity visitors. During Prohibition, Graycliff was owned by Mrs. Polly Leach, a companion to Al Capone. Later, it was purchased by Lord and Lady Dudley, Third Earl of Staffordshire, who hosted many dignitaries including Lord Beaverbrook, the Duke and Duchess of Windsor, Lord Mountbatten and Sir Winston Churchill. In 1973 Enrico and Anna Maria Garzaroli purchased Graycliff and turned the mansion into a hotel and restaurant.

Sir Winston Churchill used to stay in the Pool Cottage.

Guests can choose from old and new decor. Those with a flair for historic furnishings will like the Pool Cottage, or the Baillou, the original master bedroom in the main house. Travelers with a taste for modern decor find it in the Mandarino Cottage, which has an extra large bathroom and whirlpool tub. Rooms are air-conditioned and include a private bath. Breakfast is served to hotel guests only. The hotel is planning to expand to include eight additional guest rooms and two swimming pools.

Graycliff is an excellent choice for those seeking a sophisticated atmosphere and great dining.

NASSAU MARRIOTT RESORT & CRYSTAL PALACE CASINO
Cable Beach
☎ 242/327-6200, fax 242/327-6801
Reservations: ☎ 800/222-7466
www.marriott.com
Moderate to Expensive

Cable Beach's largest hotel is tough to miss. The 867-room property literally glows in the dark, with colored lights over each balcony giving the hotel the look of a seaside candy cane. This is one of the liveliest nightspots in town, thanks to its super-sized casino and glitzy revue.

THE OCEAN CLUB
Paradise Island Drive
Paradise Island
☎ 242/363-3000, fax 242/363-3703
Reservations: ☎ 800/321-3000
www.sunint.com
Expensive to Deluxe

This ultra-elegant resort attracts the rich and famous.

The resort has entertained Ronald Reagan, Sean Connery, Michael Caine, Sidney Poitier, Magic Johnson, and many other celebrities. The estate was first named Shangri-la, purchased in 1962 by Huntington Hartford, heir to the Great Atlantic and Pacific Tea Company fortune. The estate had formal Versailles-inspired gardens and statues of Napoleon's Josephine, FDR, David Livingstone and other historical figures. Hartford built a 51-room resort and restaurant and renamed what was then Hog Island as Paradise Island.

In 1994, Sun International (the same company that owns Atlantis and South Africa's Sun City) purchased and renovated Ocean Club from tip to toe. The hotel now offers 71 guest rooms, including four suites and five two-bedroom villas, each with a private whirlpool. All accommodations in the main building have central air-conditioning, indoor ceiling fans, outdoor ceiling fans on balconies or patios, mini-bars, safes and 27-inch televisions.

At press time this property was undergoing a major renovation; look for $40 million worth of improvements that include three new luxury villas, 54 new rooms, a new beachfront restaurant and fitness center.

RADISSON CABLE BEACH
Cable Beach
☎ 242/327-6000, fax 242/327-6987
Reservations: ☎ 800/333-3333
www.radisson.com/nassaubs_cable
Moderate to Expensive

Sporting a $15 million renovation, the Radisson Cable Beach boasts round-the-clock action both on and off the beach. Every room in the high-rise hotel offers an ocean view.

◆ **TIP**

Splurge for a junior suite, located at the end of each floor. We did and enjoyed sunrise from the bedroom balcony and sunset from the living room balcony.

A shopping arcade (with surprisingly good prices, we found) connects the Radisson with the Marriott Crystal Palace Casino.

The hotel's all-inclusive program, Splash, requires that guests wear a wristband that allows them unlimited use of all sports, plus all meals, drinks, snacks and tips.

Radisson Cable Beach offers a fun vacation atmosphere with lots of activities.

SANDALS ROYAL BAHAMIAN RESORT AND SPA
Cable Beach
☎ 242/327-6400, fax 242/327-6961
Reservations: ☎ 800/SANDALS
www.sandals.com
Expensive to Deluxe (All-inclusive)

This luxurious Sandals property offers couples a romantic, elegant atmosphere with all the options of all-inclusives, including a full menu of watersports fun.

A highlight of this resort is its excellent spa. Guests can purchase spa treatments à la carte or in packages, selecting from facials, massages, body scrubs and aromatherapy and reflexology treatments. Manicures, pedicures, paraffin hand and foot treatments, and more are also available.

Sandals is a couples-only resort.

SOUTH OCEAN GOLF AND BEACH RESORT
South Ocean
☎ 242/362-4391, fax 242/362-4310
Reservations: ☎ 800/252-7466
Moderate

For real peace and quiet, this is the place to be on New Providence. Located by itself on a wide swath of beach, South Ocean Golf and Beach Club is ideal for

*South Ocean
is a top choice
of golfers who
want to get
away from the
crowds found
in Nassau and
on Paradise
Island.*

travelers who don't want the hustle and bustle of shops and casinos (or who are content with taking the hotel van to Nassau for a day of activity).

Accommodations here include rooms in the main house and on the beach, our choice. These rooms are decorated with Caribbean furnishings and pencil post beds, and have balconies or patios that look directly out to the shallow sea.

Best Places to Eat

Cacique Award

The chefs of the Bahamas are now being recognized for their culinary skills with the Cacique Award Hotel Chef of the Year. Cacique is a word which meant "chieftain" to the Lucayan Indians who first inhabited the Bahamas. Every year the Ministry of Tourism recognizes those who have made outstanding contributions to the hospitality industry with Cacique Awards and a special category recognizes the top hotel chefs.

Price Scale - Dining

Based on a three-course dinner for one person. Prices are given in US dollars.

Expensive . . . . $40+ per person
Moderate. . . . . $25-$40
Inexpensive . . . . Under $25

Restaurants

THE AMICI RESTAURANT
Radisson Cable Beach
☎ 242/327-6000
Moderate to Expensive
Dress code: casually elegant
Reservations: suggested

Traditional Italian cuisine is the specialty of the house at this romantic two-story garden dining room with two wooden gazebos, mahogany columns, marble floors and a handpainted ceiling. The restaurant also boasts an extensive wine list.

ANDROSIA STEAK AND SEAFOOD RESTAURANT
Cable Beach Shoppers Haven
☎ 242/327-7805
Expensive
Dress code: casually elegant
Reservations: suggested

The specialty of this dinner-only restaurant is peppersteak au Paris, prepared using an heirloom recipe from Les Halles in Paris. This unique recipe uses only the best meat and a sauce that combines Dijon mustard, cracked peppercorns, brandy and a light cream sauce. Other favorites here include Bahamian grouper, red snapper, lobster thermidor, fillet of flounder, shrimp and veal.

ANTHONY'S CARIBBEAN GRILL
East Casino Drive, Paradise Island
☎ 242/363-3152
Inexpensive to Moderate
Dress code: casual
Reservations: optional

Located in the Paradise Village Shopping Centre, this fun-loving restaurant serves Bahamian and American dishes as well as some Jamaican favorites, such as pasta rasta. Families are welcome with a special kids menu; indoor and outdoor dining is available. Anthony's is a member of the Real Taste of the Bahamas program (see page 279).

ATLAS BAR AND GRILL
Atlantis, Paradise Island
☎ 242/636-3000
Moderate
Dress code: casual
Reservations: not required

Part of the new Royal Towers at Atlantis, this bar and grill offers a range of appetizers and entrées that are more than the usual snack fare.

Located just steps from the casino floor, a meal here is a fun way to start the evening. The restaurant is casual and family-friendly with a video bar and views of the new yacht marina.

Menu selections: double grilled pork chop with caramelized apple, shrimp scampi with garlic, tomato and buttered noodles.

AVERY'S RESTAURANT
Adelaide Village off Carmichael Road
☎ 242/362-1547
Inexpensive to Moderate
Dress code: casually elegant
Reservations: optional

Avery's is A Real Taste of the Bahamas member.

This restaurant serves Bahamian cuisine from souse to peas and rice and is well known for its conch fritters. The restaurant is located on South West Bay and offers free transportation from the southwest side of the island.

AVOCADO'S
Radisson Cable Beach
☎ 242/327-6000
Expensive
Dress code: dressy
Reservations: required

This fine dining restaurant features an elegant decor, candlelit tables and a romantic atmosphere. California, "Floribbean" and Bahamian influences are seen on its eclectic menu.

BACCARAT
Sandals Royal Bahamian Resort & Spa
Cable Beach
☎ 242/327-6400
All-Inclusive
Dress code: casually elegant
Reservations: required

Classical French gourmet dishes are served overlooking the pool at this fine eatery. The setting is as elegant as the meal itself, with tall, soaring windows that take in the beauty of this beachside resort.

Menu selections include grilled honey breast of duck served with chanterelles in a port wine sauce; pan-seared veal chops served in a three-peppercorn sauce and candied pearl onions; tube pasta stuffed with smoked chicken, ricotta cheese and fresh herbs with a bacon and fontina cheese sauce; sautéed sea scallops in a Chablis cream sauce with shiitake mushrooms and baked in fluffy puff pastry.

BAHAMIAN CLUB
Atlantis, Paradise Island
☎ 242/636-3000
Expensive
Dress code: dressy
Reservations: required

Nassau & New Providence Island

Baccarat is a good place for a romantic evening out.

This elegant eatery, filled with dark woods and white tablecloths, serves up steaks and seafood nightly. Prime rib is a specialty.

BAHAMIAN KITCHEN
Trinity Place off Market or Bay Streets
☎ 242/325-0702
Inexpensive
Dress code: casually elegant
Reservations: optional

The Bahamian Kitchen is a member of A Real Taste of the Bahamas.

Bahamian cuisine is the order of the day. Island delights include pan-fried turtle steak prepared with sherry and onions; okra soup and white rice; and numerous dishes featuring Bahamian seafood.

BLACK ANGUS GRILLE
Nassau Marriott Resort & Crystal Palace Casino
Cable Beach
☎ 242/327-6200, ext. 6861
Expensive
Dress code: dressy, jackets required
Reservations: required

This dinner-only restaurant serves steaks and seafood in an elegant atmosphere.

BUENA VISTA
Delancy Street
☎ 242/322-2811
Moderate to Expensive
Dress code: dressy, jacket suggested
Reservations: suggested

Buena Vista is a member of the Real Taste of the Bahamas program.

Both continental and Bahamian cuisine is featured at Buena Vista, a good choice for a special evening out. Menu offerings include such specialties as Bahamian lobster; red snapper with honey mustard; and rack of spring lamb Provencale. An extensive wine list is offered.

The restaurant is housed in a historic 19th-century mansion and has been serving vacationers and residents since 1946.

CAFE GOOMBAY
Sandals Royal Bahamian Resort and Spa
Cable Beach
☎ 242/327-6400
All-inclusive
Dress code: casually elegant
Reservations: required

This traditional Bahamian restaurant is located on the offshore island of Balmoral and is decorated in the brilliant colors of Junkanoo.

Start with an appetizer of Abaco pan-fried crab cake, conch fritters, or a Goombay roll stuffed with strips of conch. Excellent soups include Spanish Wells conch chowder or Exuma gumbo. Entrées also showcase the local catch with such dishes as conchy delight, a cracked conch fried to tender perfection, steamed tenderized conch coated with a smoked barbecue tomato coulis, snapper with a honey, peanut,and sesame seed crust served with pesto sauce and minced crawfish sautéed with scallions and basil. Desserts also reflect local tastes. Try the guava duff, coconut tart or the chocolate bread pudding.

A meal at the open-air Café Goombay is a fun experience.

CAFE JOHNNY CANOE
West Bay Street on Cable Beach
☎ 242/327-3373
Moderate
Dress code: casually elegant
Reservations: accepted only for groups

This is one of our favorite Bahamian restaurants both for its festive atmosphere and its excellent food and service. Don't look for anything fancy; this is a diner-style restaurant decorated with Bahamian crafts and photos of the restaurant's long history.

Café Johnny Canoe is a fun eatery – one of our favorites!

Café Johnny Canoe is a member of the Real Taste of the Bahamas program.

You can choose from seating indoors and outside (recommended on warm evenings, when you can share a drink beneath the multi-colored Christmas lights and listen to live music).

Breakfast, lunch and dinner are served in this popular eatery. We opted for an appetizer of conch fritters followed by grouper entrées. Prime rib, Bahamian fried chicken, fried shrimp, cracked conch and burgers round out the extensive menu. Follow it all with a Bahamian guava duff with light rum sauce.

CAFE MATISSE
Bank Lane, behind Parliament Square
☎ 242/356-7012
Moderate
Dress code: proper attire required for dinner
Reservations: suggested

Why is this charming eatery named for Matisse? Because you'll find prints of his colorful work decorating the walls. Here the real art, though, is found on the plate in the form of Italian dishes, including homemade pasta, seafood and pizza. Open for lunch and dinner.

CAFFE DEL OPERA
Bay Street
☎ 242/356-6118
Moderate
Dress code: casually elegant or dressy
Reservations: suggested

At Caffé del Opera you can order almost any dish by calling a day in advance.

This historic building, built a century ago, was once a church. Today the gospel music has been replaced by Italian opera, a perfect accompaniment to the regional Italian dishes that make this restaurant popular. Sicilian cuisine is the specialty of the house, served along with a full seafood menu. Fresh, home-made pasta is always served.

THE CAVE
Atlantis, Paradise Island
Paradise Island
☎ 242/363-3000
Inexpensive
Dress code: casual
Reservations: not required

The Cave is a fun lunch spot for families.

The fun thing about eating in this casual burger and lunchtime diner is the setting. The entire restaurant is an authentic recreation of an actual Bahamian cave. Located just steps from the waterfalls and play area, this supercasual eatery is popular with families taking a quick break from the sun.

THE CELLAR
11 Charlotte Street
☎ 242/322-8877
Inexpensive
Dress code: casual
Reservations: optional

Bahamian and continental dishes are served at this restaurant, which served as a home at the turn of the century. Quiche, salads, pasta and sandwiches make light lunches, served Monday through Saturday in the restaurant and garden patio.

CHIPPIE'S WALL ST. CAFE
Bay Street (above Cameo Factory next to the Bahamas International Stock Exchange)
☎ 242/356-2087
Inexpensive
www.chippieswsc.com

Wondering about the e-mail that's stacking up during your vacation? Just can't stay away from the Web for too long? Then head to Chippie's which,

Nassau & New Providence Island

along with sandwiches and Bahamian food, offers internet services at a cost of $8 per hour or portion of an hour. We had lunch here on a recent visit and found the place charming. It's just a few steps from the hustle and bustle of Bay Street and a good place to hop into after a morning of shopping. (It's easy to miss with its upstairs location, but worth the effort.) We had sandwiches (you'll find everything from a BLT to grilled chicken to tuna salad on the menu); other popular offerings are vegetarian quiche, conch chowder, conch salad, conch fritters (see a pattern developing here?) and seafood catch of the day. Afternoon tea is served with finger sandwiches, fresh baked scones, tea or coffee. We sat out on the front porch, a good place to watch the flurry of activity below with a cold tropical beverage in hand.

Chippie's is a must for Web heads!

COLUMBUS TAVERN
Paradise Island Drive, Paradise Island
☎ 242/363-2543
Moderate to Expensive
Dress code: casually elegant
Reservations: recommended

This nautically themed harborside restaurant offers an excellent view of vessels coming and going. Offerings include lobster flambé, steak Diane and many seafood delights.

COMFORT ZONE
#5 Wulff Road
☎ 242/323-2676
Inexpensive
Dress code: casually elegant
Reservations: optional

Comfort Zone is a member of the Real Taste of the Bahamas program.

American and Bahamian dishes bring in diners to this fun eatery. Choose from Bahamian favorites such as boiled fish, Bahamian-style potato salad, johnny cake, peas 'n rice, potato bread, souse and more.

COMPASS POINT RESTAURANT
Compass Point
West Bay Street, Gambier
☎ 242/327-4500
Moderate
Dress code: casually elegant
Reservations: suggested

The Compass Point Restaurant is one of our favorites!

This oceanfront restaurant serves inventive cuisine using local ingredients. The restaurant, an open-air seaside eatery, is as delightfully casual as the resort itself, the perfect place to throw on a colorful sundress and enjoy a Bahamian meal while listening to the sound of the surf.

Chef Stephen Bastian's talents are showcased on a menu that features Californian-Caribbean cuisine. Breakfast, lunch and dinner are served.

CONCH FRITTERS BAR AND GRILL
Marlborough Street
☎ 242/343-8778
Inexpensive
Dress code: casual
Reservations: not required

They say they have "the best conch fritters in town," so try them out. Both Bahamian and American dishes are served in a casual atmosphere.

Conch Fritters Bar and Grill is a member of the Real Taste of the Bahamas program.

THE CRYSTAL ROOM
Sandals Royal Bahamian Resort and Spa
Cable Beach
☎ 242/327-6400
All-inclusive
Dress code: casually elegant
Reservations: suggested

Nassau & New Providence Island

Elegant international fare is served à la carte at this restaurant.

Like the resort itself, The Crystal Room is for couples only.

Menu selections include marinated roast loin of pork with mustard and Cajun spices, served with a cracked peppercorn jus; grilled leg of lamb with local spices served with fresh mint and a roasted onion coulis; baby spinach, plum tomato and three cheese lasagna; tube pasta cooked al dente and served with a rich creamy sauce, roast pancetta bacon and parmesan cheese sauce.

THE DROP OFF PUB
Bay Street
☎ 242/322-3444
Inexpensive
Dress code: casual
Reservations: optional

This pub serves up both English and Bahamian versions of pub grub, from fish 'n chips to peas 'n rice. A favorite with late-night eaters (the kitchen stays open until 6 am), this spot really rocks in the evenings when sports TV and dancing bring in the crowds.

FIVE TWINS
Atlantis, Paradise Island
☎ 242/636-3000
Expensive
Dress code: casually elegant or dressy
Reservations: suggested

This elegant eatery has an eclectic menu that features Asian dishes with a gourmet twist.

Menu selections include sweet and spicy lamb with white beet, red chard and spinach pouri; crispy lobster tail with tomato-fennel-infused vegetable dressing and soba noodles; steamed seabass with oven-baked eggplant and cardamom-carrot juice;

grilled filet of beef with quick-seared bean sprouts and ginger-saffron jus; hot and sour duck breast with rosemary essence, grilled pineapple and sticky rice cake; skewered grilled salmon with tandoori-baked cauliflower and green mango chutney; calamari noodles with wok-charred squid, chorizo and endive; prawn curry with coconut broth, caramelized bok choy and silken tofu; wasabi caviar ravioli with parsnip and celery-ginger jus.

THE FORGE
Radisson Cable Beach
☎ 242/327-6000
Moderate
Dress code: casually elegant
Reservations: suggested

Ready for a little home cooking? Here's your chance to show off your own culinary skills. Guests are seated around a table-top grill and can prepare their own steaks, seafood or chicken.

FLAMINGO GARDENS CAFE
109 Collins Avenue
☎ 242/356-7904
Inexpensive
Dress code: casual
Reservations: not required

You can eat here or carry a meal out for a beachside picnic of crab and rice, boiled chicken, cassava, sweet potato, steamed conch, peas and grits and other local dishes.

THE FRYING PAN RESTAURANT
Wulff Road near Windsor Park
☎ 242/328-4887
Inexpensive
Dress code: casual
Reservations: not necessary

Flamingo Gardens is a member of the Real Taste of the Bahamas program.

Nassau & New Providence Island

This casual eatery, open 24 hours daily, is as Bahamian as it gets. You'll find authentic cuisine on the breakfast, lunch and dinner menu. Start the day with grits and corned beef, boiled grouper, stewed group or conch souse; have chicken wings and tuna for lunch. Dinner choices include mutton, cracked conch, snapper, grouper and more.

GAYLORDS
Dowdeswell Street
☎ 242/356-3004
Moderate
Dress code: dress, no casual attire
Reservations: requested

There's a food specialty shop next to Gaylords that sells Indian food items.

Situated in a 150-year-old Bahamian home, Gaylords is for those who want a taste of authentic Indian (not West Indian) cuisine. Tandoori and Indian dishes fill the menu.

GRAYCLIFF
West Hill Street
☎ 242/322-2797
Expensive
Dress code: dressy, jacket and tie suggested
Reservations: required

The most famous gourmet restaurant in all of the Bahamas (and some say the Caribbean), Graycliff has received numerous awards and honors. It is a member of the Chaine Des Rotisseurs, the oldest culinary association in the world, founded in 1248 by the king of France.

Graycliff alone is reason enough to schedule a trip to the Bahamas if you are serious about fine dining.

"The" place for visiting celebrities, Graycliff has drawn such stellar diners as Sean Connery, King Constantine, Princess Caroline, Barbara Mandrell, Paul Newman and Stevie Wonder. The restaurant has also been named one of the world's 10 best restaurants by *Lifestyles of the Rich and Famous*.

Other accolades include the Grand Award by *Wine Spectator* magazine for the 180,000-bottle wine cellar. The award has been bestowed on only 93 restaurants worldwide. For a treat, order a bottle of 1865 Chateau Lafitte for $16,000 or a 1795 Terrantez for $17,200. The restaurant also offers rare cognacs from the Charente region of France, including a 1788 Clos de Giffier Cognac and an 1872 Armagnac Janneau.

Graycliff is noted for having one of the best Cuban cigar collections in the world.

This five-star eatery serves gourmet Bahamian and continental dishes at gourmet prices; expect to spend about $150 for an average dinner for two.

Chef Ashwood Darville's specialties include such dishes as Bahamian crawfish in puff pastry; grouper with cream and Dijon mustard (featured in *Gourmet* magazine); roast rack of lamb marinated in Graycliff's secret recipe; and beef filet with sweet, hot, white and black peppers, cream, onions and cognac. Other menu selections include grilled spiny lobster with two sauces; Angus prime center cut sirloin steak with mushrooms; medallions of lamb in a delicate Chablis sauce; and roast duckling laced in a wild fruit sauce with Grand Marnier.

Historic Graycliff, on the National Register of Historic Places, is also an inn.

The setting is as exquisite as the cuisine, filled with antique charm and elegance from a Baccarat chandelier to photographs of King George VI at Buckingham Palace. Diners can enjoy their meal in the library dining rooms, filled with rare books.

Nassau & New Providence Island

GREEN SHUTTERS INN
48 Parliament Street
☎ 242/325-5702
Moderate
Dress code: dressy
Reservations: required

This English pub is located in a Bahamian home that dates back two centuries. You'll find plenty of pub grub here, from fish and chips to steak and kidney pie, all served in a genuine pub atmosphere.

HOUSE OF WONG
Marlborough Street
☎ 242/326-0045
Moderate
Dress code: casually elegant
Reservations: optional

The Hong Kong and New York chefs here serve a selection of Chinese dishes, including won ton soup and hot and sour soup. Lunch and dinner are served daily.

KINGFISH BLU BAR & GRILL AMERICANA
West Bay Street
☎ 242/323-2236
Moderate
Dress code: proper attire after 5 p.m.
Reservations: suggested

At Kingfish a cigar room is provided for those who enjoy an after-dinner Cuban stogie.

This restaurant offers a little of everything: Tex-Mex, Cajun, steaks, seafood and local selections. Start your evening with one of their over 20 types of martinis, then dig into a plate of sizzling fajitas, a juicy steak or fresh Bahamian lobster.

MAMA LIDDY'S PLACE
Market Street
☎ 242/328-6849
Inexpensive
Dress code: casual
Reservations: not required

Mama Liddy's is a member of the Real Taste of the Bahamas program and is a favorite with locals.

This Bahamian restaurant offers conch chowder, steamed grouper, peas 'n rice and other local specialties, all in a former Bahamian home.

MAMA LOO'S
Atlantis, Paradise Island
☎ 242/363-3000
Moderate to Expensive
Dress code: casually elegant or dressy
Reservations: suggested

This dinner-only eatery serves unique Carib-
bean-Chinese dishes. Diners can enjoy the flavorful
food under torchlight chandeliers in rattan
wingback chairs.

Mama Loo's is a good choice for ro-mancers.

Atlantis Art

While visiting the restaurants at Atlantis,
you'll notice art displayed throughout the
public spaces. Don't miss (actually you
couldn't miss) the spectacular huge glass
sculptures created by Seattle-based artist
Dale Chihuly. The "Temple of the Sun" and
"Temple of the Moon" are seen in the
Atlantis Casino; the Crystal Centerpiece is
at the Crystal Gate.

Florida-based sculptor Kathy Spalding created the Flying Fish Sculpture "Cypselurus"
seen on the Royal Walk. South African
sculptor Danie De Jager's work will be well
known to travelers who have visited Sun International's property in South Africa; there
he has 14 sculptures at Sun City. At
Atlantis, De Jager's work includes "The
Flying Horses" seen at the Porte Cochere entrance to the Royal Towers.

Nassau & New Providence Island

MONTAGU GARDENS

East Bay Street (one mile east of the Paradise Island Bridge)

☎ 242/394-6347

Moderate

Dress code: casually elegant

Reservations: suggested

Montagu Gardens is a member of the Real Taste of the Bahamas program.

This elegant restaurant offers such grilled specialties as blackened grouper, grilled grouper with wine sauce and filet mignon with mushrooms. The restaurant is located in a former Bahamian home on Lake Waterloo.

MURRAY'S DELI

Atlantis, Paradise Island

☎ 242/636-3000

Inexpensive

Dress code: casual

Reservations: not required

Thanks to the new Royal Towers at Atlantis, Nassau now has a genuine deli. Menu selections include grilled knochwurst with sauerkraut; burger with selected spices on kaiser roll; New York-style frankfurter; ranch burger with bacon and Swiss cheese; and hot roast beef with sweet peppers au jus. You can start the day with breakfast or come back later for more serious fare. Late-night dining is another option, with service until 6 a.m.

The deli also has an ice cream parlor with gelato, granita, designer sodas, cookies and candies.

PASSIN' JACKS RESTAURANT

East Bay Street (a half-mile east of the Paradise Island Bridge)

☎ 242/394-3245

Inexpensive to Moderate

Dress code: casually elegant

Reservations: optional

Bahamian specialties are the name of the game at this harborside restaurant – broiled grouper, cracked conch and chowder – as well as American favorites such as fajitas and steaks.

Passin' Jacks is a member of the Real Taste of the Bahamas program.

This is a good family-friendly choice.

PLANET HOLLYWOOD
Bay Street at East Street
☎ 242/325-STAR
Moderate
Dress code: casual
Reservations: required

With its outrageous noise level and location-to-location sameness, this is definitely not our favorite choice as a dining spot. However, it is popular with many visitors.

THE POOP DECK
East Bay Street just east of Paradise Island Bridge
☎ 242/393-8175
Inexpensive to moderate
Dress code: casual
Reservations: optional

This longtime favorite was the first place we ate in the Bahamas many years ago and remains one of our favorites to this day.

The Poop Deck is a member of the Real Taste of the Bahamas program.

Start with a Bahamian cocktail (or order a bottle from the extensive wine list) then move on to traditional Bahamian food. Conch chowder, grouper fingers, conch salad, cracked conch, Bahamian lobster – the list goes on. This is one of the best places for Bahamian seafood on the island.

THE SHOAL
Nassau Street
☎ 242/343-4400
Inexpensive
Dress code: casual
Reservations: not required

The Shoal is a member of the Real Taste of the Bahamas program.

Dine in or take out at this restaurant that specializes in Bahamian cuisine and is well known for boiled fish. Other favorites include stewed fish, cracked conch, stewed conch and a platter with conch, shrimp and grouper.

SOLE MARE
Nassau Marriott Resort & Crystal Palace Casino
Cable Beach
☎ 242/327-6200, ext. 6861
Expensive
Dress code: dressy, jackets required
Reservations: required

Sole Mare is a good choice for a special evening out.

This restaurant offers gourmet Italian fare for dinner only, Tuesday through Sunday.

SPICES
Sandals Royal Bahamian Resort & Spa
Cable Beach
☎ 242/327-6400
All-inclusive
Dress code: casually elegant
Reservations: suggested

Spices features Mediterranean and Caribbean dishes, prepared in an open kitchen so you can watch as your food is prepared. A couples-only restaurant, you'll find an intimate, quiet atmosphere here.

Menu selections include pan-fried grouper fillet with garlic and olives, capers, tomato and roast almonds; penne pasta sautéed with roast pancetta in a tomato sauce; veal scaloppini sautéed with a tomato sauce, and roast eggplant with fontina cheese.

TOI ET MOI
Harbour Bay Shopping Centre, East Bay Street
☎ 242/394-7056
Expensive
Dress code: dressy
Reservations: suggested

French food – black truffles, foie gras, petrossian fresh caviar – is served alongside Bahamian favorites prepared with a French flair. The restaurant offers a good wine list as well as selections of aged cognacs, armagnacs and calvados.

TONY ROMA'S
West Bay Street (opposite Saunders Beach),
Cable Beach
☎ 242/325-2020
Moderate
Dress code: casually elegant
Reservations: optional

Along with traditional Tony Roma's fare such as baby back ribs and barbecue, this location serves Bahamian conch chowder, conch fritters, cracked conch and other local favorites.

TRAVELLERS REST
West Bay Street, Gambier
(one mile west of Airport Road)
☎ 242/327-7633
Inexpensive
Dress code: casually elegant
Reservations: optional

This restaurant calls itself the home of the banana daiquiri, but it's also known for its Bahamian dishes, including minced crawfish, grouper, conch

Nassau & New Providence Island

Tony Roma's is a member of the Real Taste of the Bahamas program.

Travellers Rest is a member of the Real Taste of the Bahamas program.

and guava cake. The restaurant is located west of Cable Beach.

Fast Food

OK, you don't want to go all the way to the Bahamas to grab a burger and fries. However, if you're traveling with kids, that burger or those chicken fingers can be mighty needed. Here are a few options in Nassau:

- ☺ **Burger King**
  West Bay Street, ☎ 242/326-5747

- ☺ **McDonald's**
  Market Street, ☎ 242/326-5112;
  Malborough Street, ☎ 242/325-3631

- ☺ **Domino's Pizza**
  Cable Beach, ☎ 242/327-8000

- ☺ **Pizza Hut**
  The Plaza, Mackey St., ☎ 242/393-7291

- ☺ **Sbarro**
  Cable Beach, ☎ 242/327-3076

- ☺ **Subway**
  Cable Beach, ☎ 242/327-5516

Sunup to Sundown

In & Around Nassau

Nassau is filled with more activity options than any other Bahamian destination. The heart of Nassau is **Rawson Square**. Make your first stop here at the Visitors Information Center for brochures and maps before starting off on busy **Bay Street**, the shopping district. Here, gold and gems are sold down the street from straw baskets and t-shirts at the **Straw Market**, one of the most popular souvenir stops.

> ◆ **TIP**
>
> Look behind the Straw Market for a glimpse at the cruise ships that dock at Prince George Dock.

At Rawson Square, horse-drawn carriages wait for passengers who pay $10 (be prepared to negotiate) for a two-person, half-hour ride along picturesque Bay Street.

ARDASTRA GARDENS AND ZOO
Chippingham Road off West Bay Street
☎ 242/323-5806
Hours: 9 a.m. to 4:30 p.m. daily
Admission charged

Another popular attraction is the Ardastra Gardens and Zoo. The only zoo in the Bahamas, Ardastra features 300 animal species and 50 species of birds. You'll see monkeys, iguanas and marching pink flamingos. Stop here if you have time, but we felt that this is one stop that can be cut from busy itineraries. The caged animals are depressing to view, and we found the personnel here far from friendly.

BLUE LAGOON ISLAND
☎ 242/363-3577
Hours: daily
Admission charged

One of the most popular activities in Nassau is a day at Blue Lagoon Island. This "uninhabited" island lies about half an hour from the dock at Paradise Island and offers some beautiful beaches, hammocks beneath towering palms and plenty of watersports. For a charge, you can parasail, swim with stingrays or meet dolphins (make reservations early for this choice). One option includes feeding, petting and swimming with these friendly mammals. (The dolphin encounters can also be booked as a separate attraction without a day at Blue Lagoon Island by calling ☎ 242/363-1653.)

Blue Lagoon Island is only for those who want to party. It is not a destination if you're seeking peace and quiet or anything resembling privacy.

◆ **TIP**

If you do make this trip, bring a towel and, to save money, your own snorkel gear.

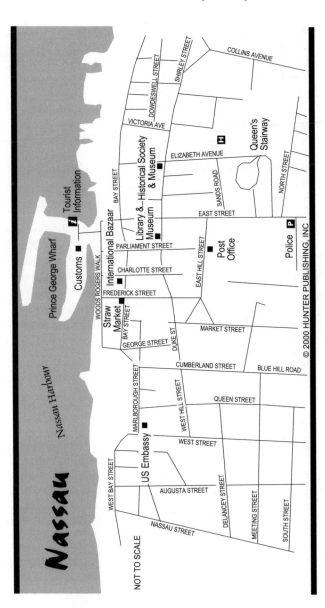

BOTANICAL GARDENS
Chippingham Road off West Bay Street
Hours: 9-4:30 weekdays, 9-4 weekends
Admission charged

A better choice for us is the nearby Botanical Gardens, where you can walk hand-in-hand along blooming paths that feature tropical plants and flowers.

CHANGING OF THE GUARD CEREMONY
Government House, Blue Hill Road
(5 minutes from downtown)
☎ 242/322-2020
Hours: fortnightly at 10 a.m.; call for specific dates
Admission: free

Just as at Buckingham Palace, the guards at Government House, representatives of Queen Elizabeth II, change shifts to the full flurry of pomp and circumstance. The Royal Bahamas Police Force Band performs at this event, which is a must-see if you're in the area.

FORT CHARLOTTE
Off West Bay Street
☎ 242/322-7500
Hours: Daily, call for hours
Admission: free

History lovers should head over to Fort Charlotte for a free guided tour of the largest fort in the Bahamas. Perched high on a hill overlooking Cable Beach, this fort never saw action, but today sees plenty of activity as tourists come to enjoy a panoramic view and a look at the fort's dungeons, cannons and exhibits.

People-to-People Program

The People-To-People program is an excellent way to learn more about Bahamian residents and culture. This program matches vacationers with more than 1,500 Bahamian volunteers for a day of activities that might include shopping at a local market, dinner with a local family, fishing, boating or a tour of back street sights. ☎ 242/326-5371, 242/328-7810 or 242/356-0435-8, fax 242/356-0434.

The **People-To-People Tea Party** is held in Nassau once a month from 4-5 p.m.; call for specific dates. Admission is free.

Another excellent way to meet local residents is at the **Government House Ballroom** for this special event. Reservations are required so check with your hotel or call the People-to-People offices (above). Proper attire is required.

POMPEY MUSEUM
Bay Street, Nassau
☎ 242/326-2566
Hours: 10-4:30 Monday to Friday, 10-1 Saturday
Admission: donation

This museum has many interesting exhibits on the emancipation of enslaved people of the Bahamas.

THE RETREAT
Village Road
☎ 242/393-1317
Hours: Tours at 11:45, Tuesday through Thursday
Admission charged

The Retreat is the home of the Bahamas National Trust. An excellent stop for nature lovers, the site offers guided tours of its native plants.

STINGRAY CITY MARINE PARK
Blue Lagoon Island
☎ 242/394-8960
Hours: Daily, 8-5:30
Admission charged

If you don't know how to dive, Stingray City offers a resort course.

This three-acre park is filled with stingrays, grouper, moray eels and tropical fish. Guests can don a mask and snorkel, swim among the marine animals and even hand-feed and pet stingrays! Scuba divers can also enjoy the park and its underwater inhabitants.

Boating & Sailing

ATLANTIS MARINA
Paradise Island
☎ 242/363-6068, fax 242/363-6008
www.sunint.com/atlantis

 This new $15 million marina can handle yachts of up to 200 feet in length. With its own 100-foot channel into Nassau Harbor, the facility offers 63 mega-yacht slips as well as 24-hour security, a ship's chandlery and dockside shopping, dock assistance for transfer of luggage and supplies, a sanitary sewer pump for each slip, daily trash pick-up, concierge services, two telephone lines and a cable television connection per slip, daily newspaper delivery, room service from Atlantis, laundry and dry cleaning.

BAREFOOT SAILING CRUISES
Bay Shore Marina
☎ 242/393-0820

This operator offers a variety of sailing cruises, from a half-day sail and snorkel (offered daily except Tuesday and Saturday) to an all-day island cruise that includes a barbecue lunch. Dinner cruises and champagne cocktail cruises are also available.

POWERBOAT ADVENTURES
Marina Harbor View, East Bay
☎ 242/327-5385

Here's a fun way to sample other Bahamian islands. A powerboat whisks you to the Exuma Cays to snorkel and see iguanas on Allen's Cay. A Bahamian lunch is provided. In the afternoon, participants can take a nature walk or feed stingrays.

THRILLER POWERBOAT TOURS
Marina at Atlantis, Paradise Island
☎ 242/363-4685
www.thrillerboat.com

These boat rides are, well, thrilling, thanks to their high speed. Tours take a half-hour to go around Paradise Island, Cable Beach or one of the other islands near Nassau. The boats depart from the Atlantis Marina but pick-up from Nassau Harbour and Cable Beach is also available. You can also charter one of these vessels for some Out Island excursions, catered lunches, snorkel trips and more.

Nassau & New Providence Island

⚠ WARNING

Thriller Powerboat rides are not suitable for pregnant women or children under five years old.

Golf

PARADISE ISLAND GOLF COURSE
☎ 800/321-3000 or 242/363-3925

Designed by Dick Wilson, the Paradise Island 18-hole course is par 72.

SOUTH OCEAN GOLF COURSE
☎ 800/223-6510 or 242/362-4391

Designed by Joe Lee, this course has 18 holes and is par 72.

CABLE BEACH GOLF COURSE
☎ 800/451-3103

Designed by Jim McCormick, this 18-hole course has 13 lakes and 50 sand traps. Par 72.

Hot, Hot, Hot

The tropical sun can get mighty toasty and you should take extra precautions against heatstroke, especially while taking part in strenuous activities. The first concern is heat cramps, muscle cramps caused because of lost water and salt. From there, it's not far to heat exhaustion, when the body tries to cool itself off and the victim feels, well, exhausted and even nauseous. Finally, heat stroke can set in, a life-threatening condition. What can you do to avoid it?

◎ **Drink water**, lots of water. Don't wait until you're thirsty to reach for the water jug. Thirst is an early sign of heat stress so start drinking before it reaches that point.

- ◎ **Slow down**. Curtail your activities whenever possible and do as the animals do in the heat – move slowly.

- ◎ Take lots of **breaks**.

- ◎ **Avoid direct sun**. Make sure you are protected. Wear wide- brimmed hats and caps as well as sunglasses.

- ◎ Wear high SPF **sunscreen**.

- ◎ Avoid the hours between 10 a.m. and 2 p.m., when the sun's rays are the strongest. Enjoy an early morning hike.

Fishing

CHUBASCO CHARTERS
East Bay Street
☎ 242/324-FISH
E-mail: chubasco@100jamz.com

Sportsfishing is the name of the game with this charter company. It offers the best fishing equipment, including Penn International Reels and Palm Beach Rods, as well as tackle. Both private and group charters are available in one of the four vessels (everything from a 34-foot Trojan to a 48-foot Hatteras).

Ask Captain Russell at Chubasco about Troy Aikman's fishing excursions with the company.

BORN FREE CHARTERS
Paradise Island
☎ 242/363-2003

This charter company specializes in deep-sea fishing and provides all necessary equipment. They're located just under the Paradise Island Bridge on the west side.

Scuba Diving

New Providence Island has many good dive sites, most found either east of Paradise Island or off the southwest coast of the island. Boat trips to the sites are fairly short.

Underwater Nassau

Nassau has long been a favorite with the movie world. Thanks to several James Bond flicks, you just might recognize some underwater sights. Nassau's marine world has starred in: *Thunderball, Never Say Never Again, Dr. No, 20,000 Leagues Under the Sea, Splash!* and *Cocoon*.

DIVERS HAVEN
East Bay Street
☎ 242/393-0869

This PADI facility offers three dives daily. Sites include the Blue Hole, wrecks and some of the places used in the James Bond movies. Complimentary shuttle service from island hotels as well as cruise ships is offered.

◆ **TIP**

If you want to learn to scuba dive, Divers Haven offers open-water certification and has daily novice scuba classes.

BAHAMA DIVERS
East Bay Street in the Yacht Haven Marina
☎ 242/393-5644

This facility offers three dives daily, daily resort classes, complimentary bus service and more. This is a PADI facility.

DIVE DIVE DIVE LTD.
Coral Harbour
☎ 242/362-1143

This PADI, ANDI, SSI and NAUI-certified facility offers everything from resort courses and certification courses up to Nitrox and Trimix extended range dives. With three dive boats, the operator takes morning, afternoon and also private charter trips to sites such as Shark Alley, Tongue of the Ocean, the Blue Hole and the James Bond sites.

NASSAU SCUBA CENTRE
Coral Harbour
☎ 242/362-1964

This PADI facility offers two-tank dives in the morning and afternoon. Shark dives and shark suit adventures are offered along with wall dives, shipwreck excursions and trips to the Exumas and Andros.

Resort course training and certification lessons are available; they can also do open-water check-out dives for PADI, NAUI, SSI and NASDS students. Free pick-up and return to all island hotels.

Horseback Riding

HAPPY TRAILS STABLES
Coral Harbour (southwest side of island)
☎ 242/362-1820

When you're ready to head out of the city and see the peaceful side of New Providence, this is a good option if you like horseback riding. The stables offer a ride just over an hour long to some of the more remote regions of the island.

Happy Trails also features beach rides.

Tours include complimentary bus pick-up from your hotel to the island's southwest shore (budget about three hours, door to door) and no more than 10 people are accepted per tour.

Happy Trails is for kids ages nine and over only; no credit cards are accepted.

City Tours

LEISURE TRAVEL TOURS
Shirley Street Plaza
☎ 242/393-1989

A tour combining the city and Paradise Island is also available from Leisure Travel.

This tour company offers a huge variety of guided tours: city tour, country tour, catamaran cruise, sailing, beach picnic – the list goes on and on. City tours take place on air-conditioned buses and include a look at the Water Tower, Straw Market, Parliament, Governor's Mansion, and more.

Bicycle Tours

PEDAL AND PADDLE ECOADVENTURES
Fire Trail Road
☎ 242/362-2772

This company offers half- and full-day tours on off-road bicycles. All equipment and refreshments are included.

Nature Tours

BAHAMAS NATIONAL TRUST
Village Road
☎ 242/393-1317

Beyond the city limits of Nassau, bird lovers have the opportunity to see a variety of tropical birds. The Bahamas National Trust organizes monthly birding outings. Another option is to call one of the birding guides accredited by the Ministry of Tourism. For information on individual tours by knowledgeable local birders, call the Ministry of Tourism at ☎ 242/322-7500.

PEDAL AND PADDLE ECOADVENTURES
Fire Trail Road
☎ 242/362-2772

This company offers all types of eco-tours on mountain bikes, by foot on nature trails and by kayak. Half-day tours on bike or kayak include all equipment, refreshments and fresh fruit, and use of binoculars, snorkel and mask. Guides are knowledgeable.

Aerial Tours

With the proximity of islands, the Bahamas is a good destination to see on an air tour, either by helicopter or small aircraft. Several operators offer guided tours as well as aerial photography tours; call these operators for information on prices and hours:

HELI-TOURS
Paradise Island Heliport
(a quarter-mile west of the harbor)
☎ 242/363-4016

SKY UNLIMITED LIMITED
Nassau International Airport
☎ 242/377-8993 or 377-8777, fax 242/377-3107

SANDPIPER AIR AND 4 WAY CHARTER
Nassau International Airport
☎ 242/377-5751 or 377-5602, fax 242/377-3143

LE AIR CHARTER SERVICES LIMITED
Nassau International Airport
☎ 242/377-2356 or 377-2357, fax 242/377-3375

Shop Till You Drop

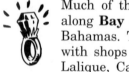

Much of the shopping in Nassau is found along **Bay Street**, the Fifth Avenue of the Bahamas. This bustling boulevard is lined with shops stocked with names like Gucci, Lalique, Cartier and Baccarat. Inside, display cases gleam with gold, diamonds and emeralds, and travelers look for duty-free bargains.

Shoppers will find this street filled with the offerings of an international bazaar: Irish linens, Columbian emeralds and French perfumes.

Perfume prices are regulated by the government, so you will find the same prices at any of the "perfume bars" which are common in Nassau.

Everything from French to American perfumes, colognes and aftershaves are sold in the perfume bars, as well as in many clothing stores.

Additional shopping (mostly upscale) is found on Paradise Island at Hurricane Hole, just over the Paradise Island Bridge and at Atlantis, Paradise Island.

How Good Is the Shopping?

Nassau is known for its world-class shopping. Baubles from around the world will tempt you. But just how good are the bargains? Do some research before you leave home to determine how real those discounts are, but expect to see the biggest savings on high-ticket items such as fine jewelry and watches. Here are some sample prices we saw during a recent shopping trip along Nassau's Bay Street:

Jewelry: 18k gold band with ½ carat small diamonds, $600; 14k gold earrings with small porpoises, $100; .75 carat diamond drop, $1,900; .50 carat diamond drop, $1,100; Carrera y Carrera Romantic Collection, Romeo and Jullietta ring, $850; 14k tanzanite and diamond ring, $4,400.

Men's Watches: Breitling 18k gold Chronomat with mother of pearl dial, $16,000; Breitling 18k gold and stainless steel, $2,900; Tag Heuer "6000" stainless tell chronometer, $1,850; Tag Heuer "Kirium" stainless steel chonograph, $1,500; Rado "Ceramica," $1,350; Omega "Seamaster" stainless steel, $1,400; Omega "Mars-Watch" titanium, $2,400; Gucci "7700" stainless steel, $675; Gucci "9045" stainless steel, $470; Raymond Weil "Parsifal" 18k gold and stainless steel, $1,400; Raymond Weil "Tango" stainless steel, $475; Raymond Weil "W1" stainless steel, $600; Yves Saint Laurent "EXP 101" cronograph, $145; Yves Saint Laurent "SNL 650" stainless steel chronograph, $750; Swiss Army "Officer" stainless steel, $233; Swiss Army "Renegade" with compass, $75; Longines "Dolve Vita" stainless steel chronograph, $950; Tissot "Ballade" 18k gold plated, $320; Tissot titanium, $360; Ebel "Topwave" 18k gold and stainless steel, $940; Ebel "Modulor" stainless steel chronograph, $2,800.

Ladies Watches: Rado "Integral Jubile" with diamond dial, $1,400; Breitling "Callistino" 18k gold and stainles steel, $1,900; Breitling "J-Class" 18k gold and stainless steel $2,800; Tag Heuer "2000 Evolution" $800; Tag Heuer "Kirium" stainless steel, $1,200; Gucci "2305" 18k gold, $600; Gucci "6700" stainless steel, $500; Rayond Weil "Chorus" 18k gold plated, $550; Yves Saint Laurent 18k gold bangle watch, $150; Yves Saint Laurent 18k gold plated mother of pearl diamond dial, $185; Swiss

Army "Officer," $300; Longines "La Grande Classique," $680; Ebel sport 18k and stainless steel with diamond dial, $3,700.

Collectibles: Lladró Angel with flute, $80; Lladró Mirage, $220; Lalique Baccantes Vase, $2,700; Lalique Chrysis paperweight, $370; Lenox five place setting dinner plates, "Autumn" design, $48; Waterford Lismore champagne flute, $44; Swarovski silver crystal miniature crab, $50; Hummel figurine "Bahamas News," $240; Royal Doulton, vase $35.

Leather goods: Versace wallet, $160; Bally black belt with silver buckle (men's), $100; Bally briefcase with silver trim, $660; Bally wallet, $120; Salvatore Ferragamo Gancini bag, $380; Salvatore Ferragamo wallet, $180.

Perfumes/fragrances: CK One, 200ml, $40; Elizabeth Arden Fifth Avenue, 125ml spray, $43; Champs Elyssées Spray (3.4oz), $39.50; Gianni Versace for women (1.6oz), $40; Poeme for women (1.7oz), $44.50; Trésor for women (1.7oz), $44.50; Organza for women (1.7oz), $44.50; Allure for women (1.7oz), $44; Hugo Spray for men (5.1oz), $49; Blue Jeans for men (2.5oz), $30; Moschino Uomo (2.5oz), $38.50; Sculpture for Men (1.7oz), $38; Pleasures for Men (1.7oz), $25; Eternity for Men (100ml spray), $36.

The Best Shops

CRYSTAL COURT
Atlantis Resort, Paradise Island

This collection of over a dozen stores is a shopper's delight. Located in the promenade just off the Atlantis Casino, this 35,000-square-foot collection of fine stores includes designs from Gucci, Bulgari, Cartier, Lalique, Versace, Ferragamo and more. There's also a Nicole Miller store with designs created especially for Atlantis.

SOLOMON'S MINES
Bay Street, ☎ 242/322-2201
Atlantis, Paradise Island, ☎ 242/363-3616
Hurricane Hole, Paradise Island, ☎ 242/363-2209
www.solomons-mines.com

This large shop sells plenty of high-priced items at good prices. Look for fine jewelry by Carrera y Carrera, crystal by Lalique and Baccarat, china by Lladro, Versace accessories and perfume by Chanel.

Fine Jewelry

COLOMBIAN EMERALDS INTERNATIONAL
Bay Street, opp. the Straw Market, ☎ 242/322-2230
Atlantis Resort, Beach Towers, ☎ 242/363-3128
Atlantis Resort, Royal Towers, ☎ 242/363-3120
Bay Street, Scotia Bank Building, ☎ 242/326-1661

This popular Caribbean boutique has locations in Antigua, Aruba, Barbados, the Cayman Islands, Grenada, St. Lucia, St. Martin, the USVI and other islands. It sells other fine gemstones. All purchases include certified appraisals, 90-day insurance and full international guarantees.

THE ORIGINAL COLOMBIAN
EMERALDS AND FINE JEWELLERY
Bay Street
☎ 242/325-4083 or 322-2766

These stores sell, yes, you guessed it, emeralds. You'll find all types of other precious stones and fine jewelry here as well. Pieces by Philippe Charriol, Chaumet and Piaget are featured.

JEWELER'S WAREHOUSE
Bay Street, opposite the Straw Market
☎ 242/322-2214

This discount jeweler advertises 50% off all jewelry and 35% off watches. You'll also find gold and silver jewelry here. This store has good prices on a variety of fine jewelry, from earrings starting under $100 and small strands of pearls for under $35 to fine gemstones that command a four-digit price tag.

What to Buy?

Nassau offers one of the best shopping selections in the entire region and most stores are located within walking distance of each other. Top purchases in Nassau are: perfumes, cosmetics, fine watches, leather goods, linens, sweaters and china.

> ◆ **TIP**
>
> You won't find equal savings on all goods so be sure to do some research before you go.

Watches

CARTIER
Bay Street
☎ 242/322-4391

This boutuque sells Cartier items exculsively. Choose from watches, belts, jewelry and more.

Nassau & New
Providence Island

JOHN BULL
Bay Street
☎ 242/322-4252

Most visitors find themselves in this shop looking for a Rolex watch because John Bull is an official Rolex retailer. If Rolex is not your sytle, choose from other upscale items such as gemstones, sunglasses and cosmetics.

SOLOMON'S MINES
Bay Street, ☎ 242/322-2201
Atlantis, Paradise Island, ☎ 242/363-3616
Hurricane Hole, Paradise Island, ☎ 242/363-2209
www.solomons-mines.com

Breitling, Omega, Rado, Tag Heuer, Gucci and Raymond Weil watches are sold at this large shop.

China, Crystal & Figurines

TREASURE TRADERS
Bay Street
☎ 242/355-8512

This shop houses one of the largest collections of Herend hand-painted china in the world, a treasure to collectors.

Cigars

HURRICANE HOLE LIQUORS & CIGAR MERCHANTS
Hurricane Hole Plaza, Paradise Island
☎ 242/363-4866

Providing visitors with international and local spirits and cigars. Bahamian, Jamaican and Cuban cigars are all for sale.

Can I Mail This Home?

If you've shopped until you dropped and loaded up on presents for the folks back home, you might consider mailing some packages instead of hauling them back through the airports and through customs. Here are the rules that govern mailings:

US: You can mail home any number of gifts duty-free as long as the recipient doesn't receive gifts totaling more than $100 in a day. You can't mail home gifts of tobacco or liquor.

You won't get duty-free/tax-free benefits on perfume that's over $5 in value. You must mark purchases "unsolicited gift" and write this on the outside of the package. You may also send items to yourself for personal use. To qualify as duty-free, these items must not be worth morth than $200.

CANADA: You can send a gift to Canada duty-free if it is worth C$40 or less. You cannot mail home gifts of tobacco, liquor or advertising matter.

UK: You can mail home gifts if you're sending them to an individual (as opposed to a company). Duty-free gifts may not be used for commercial trade. Gifts can't exceed £145.

Grog & Spirits

HURRICANE HOLE LIQUORS & CIGAR MERCHANTS
Hurricane Hole Plaza, Paradise Island
☎ 242/363-4866

This shop sells international and local spirits as well as Bahamian, Jamaican and Cuban cigars.

HARBOUR BAY LIQUORS
Harbour Bay Shopping Center
☎ 242/394-0630

Those searching for locally made liquors can find them here alongside imported wine, beer and rum.

Gifts & Souvenirs

EVERYTHING'S PARADISE
Hurricane Hole Plaza
☎ 242/363-2217

Need a gift for those left at home? Head to this souvenir shop, where you can pick up t-shirts, postcards and a host of other items.

GONE BANANAS
International Bazaar
☎ 242/323-3910

Find swimwear, sunglasses and gifts for your friends at this shop.

PARADISE TEES
Hurricane Hole Plaza on Paradise Island
☎ 242/363-2609

Bahamian crafts, jewelry, t-shirts, and more can be found here.

Cigars

GRAYCLIFF CIGAR FACTORY
West Hill Street
☎ 242/322-2796

This smoke shop sells, among countless name brand cigars, Graycliff cigars hand-rolled by Avelino Lara.

Graycliff is a must for cigar buffs.

Leather Goods

LEATHER MASTERS
Parliament Street
☎ 242/322-7597

Shop for name brand purses, wallets, belts and more by such designers as Gianni Versace and Paloma Picasso.

You'll also find designer luggage and sunglasses at Leather Masters.

BRASS & LEATHER I AND II
Charlotte Street
☎ 242/322-3806

Choose from shoes, handbags, belts and other items for both men and women.

FENDI
Bay and Charlotte Streets
☎ 242/322-6300

Italian imports can be found at Fendi – luggage, wallets, purses and briefcases. You can also purchase men's and women's watches and fragrances.

GUCCI
Bank Lane and Bay Street in Saffrey Square
☎ 242/325-0561

Genuine Gucci goods such as perfume, shoes and leather products are found at this elegant boutique.

Perfumes & Cosmetics

THE PERFUME BAR
Bay and Frederick Streets
☎ 242/325-1258

This is just one of nine Perfume Bar locations around Nassau. It sells top-of-the-line skin care products, cosmetics and perfumes.

THE PERFUME SALON
Radisson Cable Beach Shopping Mall
☎ 242/327-6666

This salon offers fragrances from around the world in addition to exclusive cosmetic lines.

Fashion Boutiques

AMERICAN CLASSICS
The Mall at Marathon
☎ 242/394-3900

This store features the American styles of Tommy Hilfiger. You'll find hats, shirts, shorts, ties, shoes and much more for men and boys here.

MADEMOISELLE
Bay Street
☎ 242/322-5130

This is where fashionable ladies come to buy the perfect outfit for a night in the Bahamas. Imported dresses, shoes, hats and bags can all be found at this elegant boutique.

FAR EAST TRADERS
Prince George Plaza
☎ 242/325-7095

If you're looking for imports from the Orient, this is the place. Kimonos, tableclothes, silks and other goodies can all be found at this unique store.

Local Crafts

STRAW MARKET
Bay Street

This two-story shopping complex is a must in Nassau, even if it's just to have a look around. The stalls here are filled with straw goods (many of them imported, although some actually produced here). Expect to haggle over prices, but keep in mind that prices and goods vary only slightly from booth to booth. Upstairs, wood carvers chip away at logs to produce sculptures of animals, birds and anything else you might request.

BAHAMACRAFT CENTRE
Paradise Island, next to Atlantis, Paradise Island

This $2.4 million complex was built by Sun International in conjunction with the Bahamian government. Here you'll find many traditional Bahamian crafts – straw goods, wood carvings, clothing, glass, specialty foods, art and jewelry.

The center, open 9 a.m. to 7 p.m. daily, is about a two-minute walk from Atlantis' Coral Tower. The market is opposite the Hurricane Hole shopping area. Major credit cards are accepted.

If you're staying at Atlantis, take the shuttle bus from the lobby to the Bahama-Craft Centre.

Nassau & New Providence Island

After Dark

Casinos

Nassau is home to casinos at the **Nassau Marriott Crystal Palace Casino and Resort**, ☎ 242/327- 6200, and the **Atlantis, Paradise Island**, ☎ 242/ 363-3000. The one at Atlantis is the largest in the Caribbean, with over 1,000 slot machines and 80 gaming tables. The casino has a nautical theme.

Nightclubs

THE ZOO
West Bay Street at Saunders Beach
☎ 242/322-7195

With a name like The Zoo, you'd expect wild nightlife and you're right. This dance club doesn't open until 8 p.m. and really gets rolling after midnight with die-hard partiers staying until 4 a.m. There's a hefty cover charge ($20-$40, depending on the night), but you can often find coupons in one of the many giveaway publications.

COCKTAILS AND DREAMS
Western Esplanade at West Bay
☎ 242/328-3745

Cocktails and Dreams' happy hour extends from noon to 8 p.m.

This casual nightclub is the only one on the beachfront. Night owls don't call it quits until 8 a.m.

COLUMBUS TAVERN
Paradise Harbour Club, Paradise Island
☎ 242/363-2534

If you're looking for a quiet evening in a tavern atmosphere, here it is. The Columbus Tavern has great views of the harbor and good beer prices.

CLUB WATERLOO
One mile east of the Paradise Island Bridge
☎ 242/393-7324

The action at this lively nightclub extends to both indoors and outside.

DICKY MO'S
West Bay Street, Cable Beach
☎ 242/327-7854

This longtime favorite on Cable Beach has a nautical atmosphere.

DRAGONS
Atlantis, Paradise Island
☎ 242/363-3000

Located in the Royal Towers, this nightclub is high-tech and high-energy. The bandstand is elevated 10 feet above the floor and the whole atmosphere is fanciful, from dragon sculptures to video montages of fire dancing and voodoo.

Theater

DUNDAS THEATRE FOR THE PERFORMING ARTS
Mackey Street
☎ 242/393-3728

This local theater offers year-round productions. It's operated by local resident David Donaldson, who has worked with Sidney Poitier and James Earl Jones and written plays for the New York Shakespeare Festival. Call for current productions.

Bahamian Shows

NATIVE'S AUTHENTIC BAHAMIAN EXPERIENCE
East Bay Street, at the
foot of Paradise Island Bridge
☎ 242/394-8280 or 394-8282

Every Thursday night this show brings you a fire eater, limbo dancer, a contortionist known as the Crab Man, and plenty of fun. You can buy a show ticket ($30) or a dinner and show combo ($50); all tickets include round-trip transfers and one tropical drink.

Children's tickets (5-11 years) are also available for the Native Bahamian show.

Shows & Revues

NASSAU MARRIOTT RESORT & CRYSTAL PALACE CASINO
Cable Beach
☎ 242/327-6200

This splashy show is performed in the casino's Rainforest Theater and is one of the largest shows in the region. You can purchase a dinner package or a ticket for the show only. Performances are on Tuesday, Wednesday, Friday and Saturday at 8:45 and 11 p.m., Thursday and Sunday at 8 p.m. The Las Vegas-style revue features flashy costumes and dancing girls, tropical music and plenty of fun.

KINGS AND KNIGHTS CLUB
Forte Nassau Beach Hotel, Cable Beach
☎ 242/327-7711

If you're looking for something more Bahamian, check out the Kings and Knights Club. For over 35 years this delightful show has entertained visitors with Bahamian songs, dances, steel bands, fire eaters, limbo dancers, comedians and even a few bawdy calypso tunes.

Comedy Clubs

JOKER'S WILD COMEDY CLUB
Atlantis Resort, Paradise Island
☎ 242/363-3000

Be sure to call for reservations at this popular comedy club, located on the main level of Atlantis. Touring comics bring both big names and new talent to the nightlclub.

Nassau A-Z

American Embassy

You can obtain assistance from the Embassy during working hours at their Nassau office on Queen Street, ☎ 242/322-1181.

American Express Office

The local American Express travel office is located at 303 Shirley Street (☎ 242/322-2931). For emergency card replacement, ☎ 800/327-1267; for lost traveler's check replacement, ☎ 800/221-7282.

Banks

Citibank
Thomas Boulevard, ☎ 242/302-8500
Frederick Street, ☎ 242/322-6800

Commonwealth Bank
Bay and Christi Streets, ☎ 242/322-1154

Barclays
Bay Street, ☎ 242/356-8000

Bridal Consultants

Want to tie the knot while you're in Nassau? Many of the larger hotels offer bridal consultants on staff; you can also obtain assistance with everything from paperwork to party favors at these offices:

En'ella Floral and Bridal
PO Box N-1577
Nassau, Bahamas
☎ 242/394-ROSE

Incredible Services
PO Box N-1507
Nassau, Bahamas
☎ 242/341-1482
E-mail: incred@batelnet.bs

Wedding Circle
Winders Terrace
Nassau, Bahamas
☎ 242/323-3549
E-mail: vikki@bahama.net.bs
www.bahamaweddingcircle.com

**Anna's Wedding Planning
& Consulting Service**
PO Box N-8611
Nassau, Bahamas
☎ 242/324-2559

Dentists

The Walk-In Dental Clinic
36 Marathon Estates Road
☎ 242/393-6588

Family Dental Centre
Mackey and Bay Streets, five minutes south of the
Paradise Island Bridge
☎ 242/325-0453 or 393-7333

Village Dental Centre
Corner Village and Brooklyn Roads
☎ 242/394-7632

Cable Beach Family Dental Care
Hoffer Plaza across from Sandals
☎ 242/327-4020

Emergency Phone Numbers

Emergencies . . . . ☎ 911
Hospital (Nassau) . . ☎ 322-2861, 322-8411
Ambulance . . . . ☎ 322-2221
Med Evac. . . . . ☎ 322-2881
Air Ambulance . . . . ☎ 327-7077
Fire . . . . ☎ 911
Police . . . . ☎ 911

Hospital

Lyford Cay Hospital
Lyford Cay, New Providence Island
☎ 242/362-4025

Doctor's Hospital
Collins Avenue and Shirley Street,
Nassau, New Providence Island
☎ 242/322-4811

Limo Service

Unlike most islands, Nassau has an extensive fleet of limousines. They're nice for touring the island in real style and great for large families or for special events. On one recent trip, we had a driver from Lil Murph and Sons; it was a great way to see the island in comfort with plenty of room for our photo gear (not to mention a big boost to our egos).

Lil Murph and Sons, ☎ 242/325-3725

D-Best Limousine and Tours, ☎ 242/393-0065

Exclusive Chauffeurs, ☎ 242/356-5900

STS Limousine Service, ☎ 242/393-5119

The Rich and Famous Limousine Service, ☎ 242/364-7326

Optical Services

Nassau Sight Centre
Ivanhoe and Winsor Roads
☎ 242/393-6533

Optique Shoppe
22 Parliament Street
☎ 242/322-3910

Centre Valley Optical (one-hour service)
70 Collins Avenue
☎ 242/322-3094

Imperial Optical Co.
Marathon Mall
☎ 242/393-5959

Pharmacies

Cole-Thompson Pharmacies
Bay and Charlotte Streets
☎ 242/322-2062

Heaven Sent Pharmacy
New Base Road Business Centre, Nassau Street
☎ 242/326-4629; emergency ☎ 242/324-6394

Pharm-Care Delivery Service
☎ 242/328-5351
Pharm-Care will deliver supplies and prescription drugs to you; you'll need your physician to call in or fax your prescription.

Super Saver Pharmacy
Marathon Mall
☎ 242/393-4293

Neighborhood Pharmacy
South Beach
☎ 242/392-7700

Photo Labs

Colour Masters
Rosetta and Patton Streets
☎ 242/356-3414

Mr. Photo
Bay Street (adjacent to the Straw Market)
☎ 242/323-8146

Shoe Repair

Shoe Medic
Mall at Marathon (near main entrance)
☎ 242/323-0358

Wilson's Department Store & Shoe Repairing
East Street and Wulff Road
☎ 242/323-4250

Beyond New Providence Island

We call this book "Nassau & The Bahamas" because what lies beyond the city lights is special as well, whether you discover it as a day trip from Nassau or as a destination in itself. In all directions, you'll find islands that offer beautiful waters and sandy beaches. Some, like Grand Bahama Island, offer the many temptations of Nassau as well – casinos, shopping, fine dining. Others, like the quiet Out Islands, have a small-town feel where you can kick back and become, at least for a few days, one of the handful of residents who call these lands home.

To the east of Nassau lie the Turks and Caicos islands, not part of the Bahamas but with many of the same features as these islands. Don't exclude these islands in a list of possible destinations, whether you're considering an all-inclusive resort stay or a visit to a small, family-operated hotel filled with returning scuba divers. You'll find more about these special islands in the Turks and Caicos chapter.

The Abacos

The Abacos aren't one destination but a whole family of little islands. Like tossed seashells, they span a 650-square-mile area.

Location

They're in the northeastern end of the Bahamas (so far to the north that they're sometimes nicknamed "The Top of the Bahamas"). They are 106 miles north of Nassau and 175 miles east of Palm Beach, Florida.

The Abacos are a favorite with sailors, yachties and anglers.

The Abacos are the second-largest island group in the Bahamas. The majority of the landforms aren't developed, but you will find many that are inhabited, including Man-O-War Cay, Great Abaco, Elbow Cay, Great Guana Cay, Treasure Cay, Green Turtle Cay, Spanish Cay and Walker Cay.

Great Abaco is on the western side of the island group, separated by the Sea of Abaco from the cays on the east.

Islands of the Abacos

Elbow Cay

Five miles east of Marsh Harbour lies Elbow Cay. The community of Hope Town overlooks the harbor and is filled with pastel-tinted houses built in a New England style. You can't miss the candy striped lighthouse built in 1863. Today it is one of the few manned lighthouses in the Bahamas.

Great Abaco

This large island is home to Marsh Harbour, the Bahamas' third-largest city. Here visitors will find plenty of shopping, nightlife, dining and watersports fun. Marsh Harbour makes a good gateway to the neighboring cays, with regular ferry service to Hope Town in Elbow Cay and to Man-O-War Cay. Marsh Harbour is one of the biggest yachting centers in the Bahamas and has a fun, yachty atmosphere.

Great Guana Cay

Located 10 miles from Marsh Harbour by boat, this laid-back island is noted for its beautiful beaches, an excellent offshore reef and good watersports.

Green Turtle Cay

One of the oldest settlements in the Abacos, Green Turtle Cay is home to New Plymouth, a colonial village that looks like something right out of a time warp. New England-style buildings dot the island's southern tip, a reminder of those early British Loyalists who relocated here. Green Turtle Cay is situated just east of Treasure Cay and is popular with those looking for watersports, gamefishing and bonefishing.

Little Harbour

This cay was once accessible only by boat, but today drivers can come to this charming island via road from Marsh Harbour. Diving, snorkeling, shelling and cave exploring are all found here.

The Abacos

Man-O-War Cay

From Marsh Harbour you can take a ferry out to Man-O-War Cay, the top boat-building area in the Abacos. Not only do full-size boats and yachts come to this region, but collectors also venture here to visit Joe Albury. For generations, Albury's family has created sailing dinghies and gifts in the studio, all crafted from Abaco hardwoods.

Man-O-War Cay is known as the "nautical capital" of the Abacos.

The atmosphere on Man-O-War is very family-oriented, with a more formal dress than on many of the other islands and no liquor stores.

Spanish Cay

Spanish Cay is popular with anglers and divers.

Treasure Cay

Treasure Cay is home to the only 18-hole championship golf course in the Abacos.

Accessible by boat or car from Marsh Harbour, Treasure Cay is the second most populated area on Great Abaco. The island includes condominiums, resorts and visitor facilities.

Walker's Cay

This ritzy island has been featured in many publications and is a favorite with anglers, divers and yachties.

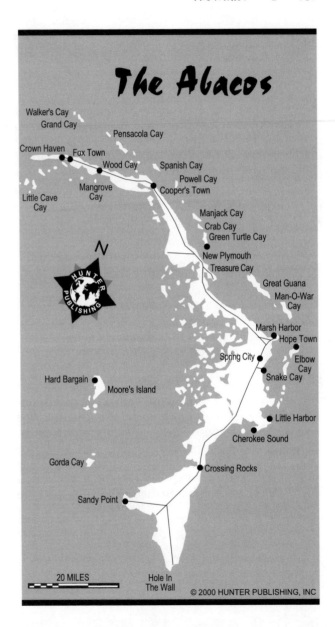

The Abacos

Walker's Cay
Grand Cay
Pensacola Cay
Crown Haven
Fox Town
Wood Cay
Spanish Cay
Powell Cay
Cooper's Town
Mangrove Cay
Little Cave Cay
Manjack Cay
Crab Cay
Green Turtle Cay
New Plymouth
Treasure Cay
Great Guana
Man-O-War Cay
Marsh Harbor
Hope Town
Spring City
Elbow Cay
Snake Cay
Hard Bargain
Moore's Island
Little Harbor
Cherokee Sound
Gorda Cay
Crossing Rocks
Sandy Point
20 MILES
Hole In The Wall

© 2000 HUNTER PUBLISHING, INC

History

The history of these islands is an interesting one. After the American Revolution, disenchanted British Loyalists moved here from New England and the Carolinas, bringing with them New England building styles. They also brought with them boat-building skills, and soon adapted those skills to include pirating.

Nearly 500 Spanish galleons rest on Abaco's ocean floor.

★ DID YOU KNOW?

Today, that pirate legacy has resulted in many good scuba diving sites, including Devil's Hole, eight miles north of Treasure Cay, and the Pelican Cay National Park, located between Lynyard Cay and Tilloo Cay south of Marsh Harbour, a 2,000-acre park.

The pirating days came to an end in the mid-1800s when the Abaconians built the first lighthouses. The descendants of those early residents never forgot their ties to the Mother Country. In 1972, when the Bahamas asked for independence from Britain, the Abaconians petitioned Queen Elizabeth II to allow their islands to remain a British colony. The petition was not granted.

Best Places to Stay

Price Scale - Accommodations

*Based on a standard room for two in high
season. Prices are given in US dollars.*

Deluxe	$300+
Expensive	$200-$300
Moderate	$100-$200
Inexpensive	Under $100

ABACO BEACH RESORT & BOAT HARBOUR MARINA

Marsh Harbour
☎ 242/367-2158, fax 242/367-2819
Reservations: ☎ 800/468-4799
E-mail: abrandbh@batelnet.bs
www.greatabacobeach.com
Moderate

This resort offers 52 oceanfront rooms and six
two-bedroom cottages, each with either private ter-
races or oceanview balconies. Rooms have air conditioning, mini-refrigerator, wet bar, coffee maker,
satellite TV, hair dryer and, in the cottages, a full
kitchen.

Other amenities include a dive site, grocery store, liquor store and a 180-slip marina, the largest in the
Bahamas. The marina caters to vessels up to 200
feet and has cable TV and telephone hookups for the
largest slips.

*One pool at
Abaco Beach
Resort has a
swim-up bar.*

Guests can also enjoy a private beach, two pools,
tennis, bicycle rentals and the Angler's Restaurant.

The Abacos

BANYAN BEACH CLUB
Treasure Cay
☎ 888/625-3060, 242/365-8111, fax 242/365-8226
www.banyanbeach.com
Moderate

This beachside hideaway offers condominiums with two or three bedrooms. They're located on "one of the 10 best beaches in the world," according to *National Geographic*. When you've had your fill of strolling the white sand beach, you can play tennis or golf, or go scuba diving, fishing or shopping, all of which are nearby.

BLUFF HOUSE CLUB AND MARINA
Green Turtle Cay
☎ 242/365-4257, fax 242/365-4248
E-mail: bluffhouse@oii.net
www.oii.net/BluffHouse
Inexpensive to Deluxe

True upscale elegance is found at this resort which offers 28 guest rooms and villas. All rooms have refrigerators, coffee makers and hair dryers. The resort has an excellent gourmet restaurant called the Bluff House Restaurant.

COCO BAY COTTAGES
P.O. Box AB-795
Green Turtle Cay
☎ 242/365-5464, fax 242/365-5465
Reservations: ☎ 800/752-0166
E-mail: cocobay@oii.net
www.oii.net/cocobay
Moderate to Expensive

The cottages at Coco Bay are perfect for families.

Four two- and-three bedroom cottages make up this quiet hideaway that's a favorite with those looking to get away and enjoy bonefishing, snorkeling and diving. This casual getaway is a good choice for those who want to make their own fun.

CONCH INN MARINA AND HOTEL

Marsh Harbour, Great Abaco
☎ 242/367-4000, fax 242/367-4004
Reservations: ☎ 800/688-4752
Inexpensive

This small hotel has just nine rooms, but is adjacent to one of the area's best marinas. Operated by The Moorings, the largest charter yacht company in the world, Conch Inn Marina is often used by those coming to charter a vessel either the night of their arrival or the night before their departure. Rooms include cable TV and air conditioning and there's access to a freshwater pool.

HOPE TOWN HIDEAWAYS LTD.

Hope Town, Elbow Cay
☎ 242/365-0224, fax 242/366-0434
Reservations: ☎ 800/688-4752
www.hopetown.com
Moderate

These villas have all the comforts of home: telephone, air conditioning, a full kitchen and even a private dock.

TREASURE CAY HOTEL RESORT AND MARINA

Treasure Cay
☎ 957/525-7711, fax 954/525-1699
Reservations: ☎ 800/327-1584
E-mail: abaco@gate.net
www.treasurecay.com
Moderate

Treasure Cay Resort is home to an 18-hole championship golf course designed by Dick Wilson and rated at par 72. The resort also boasts a 150-slip marina and is situated on an incredible white sand beach. Other amenities include tennis, a freshwater pool, dive shop, bicycle rentals and more.

The Abacos

Golfers will appreciate the beachside Treasure Cay Resort.

Best Places to Eat

Price Scale - Dining

Based on a three-course dinner for one person. Prices are given in US dollars.

Expensive. . . . . $40+
Moderate. $25-$40
Inexpensive . . . . Under $25

ANGLER'S RESTAURANT
Abaco Beach Resort and Boat Harbour
☎ 242/367-2871
Moderate
Dress code: casually elegant
Reservations: recommended

This waterside restaurant overlooks Boat Harbour Marina and serves international cuisine with island flair. Breakfast starts the day with traditional bacon and egg offerings as well as Belgian waffles, French toast, corned beef hash and smoked salmon. Lunch choices include chicken wings with blue cheese dip, coconut-mango shrimp with fruit chutney and conch fritters.

Dinner is a more elegant affair, with linen tablecloths and candles. Evening menu offerings include fresh shrimp, grouper and scallops tossed with red or white sauce and served with creamy risotto; an island seafood cake with grilled shrimp sparked by avocado chutney; and sushi prepared using the day's catch.

BJ'S RESTAURANT AND BAR
Mount Hope
Little Abaco
☎ 242/365-2205
Inexpensive
Dress code: casual
Reservations: not required

This local diner serves Bahamian dishes in a casual atmosphere. Breakfast starts the day rolling here with local favorites such as boiled fish with johnny cake, chicken souse, eggs and grits or French toast. The lunch menu offers burgers and sandwiches. The evening hours bring plenty of action, with live entertainment and dancing.

There's nothing fancy about the setting at BJ's; people come here for the food.

Menu selections include cracked conch, fried or steamed chicken, steamed turtle, grouper fingers, barbecued ribs, steamed fish, curried chicken and beef ribs.

BLUFF HOUSE RESTAURANT
Green Turtle Cay
☎ 242/365-4247
Expensive
Dress code: dressy
Reservations: required

Gourmet dinners served by soft candlelight in the historic main house bring romantics to this restaurant. Recently renovated to its historic splendor, the Bluff House Restaurant offers up to five entrée selections every night from 7:30 p.m. Breakfast is also served.

Breakfast at Bluff House may be eaten indoors or outside on the patio by the pool.

Menu offerings include Bahamian grouper filet coated in a tomato and basil sauce and topped with melted mozzarella cheese; crispy duck breast served with a grapefruit and Grand Marnier sauce; fillet mignon Forestier served with a mushroom, bacon and parsley sauce; Bahamian lobster tail with a spe-

The Abacos

cial lemon and butter sauce; and roast loin of lamb wrapped in bacon and served with a honey and rosemary glaze.

CAP'N JACK'S
Hope Town
☎ 242/366-0247
Inexpensive to Moderate
Dress code: casual
Reservations: optional

Cap'n Jack's offers special kid's meals.

This large white house sits right on the harborfront. The restaurant and bar offers Bahamian dishes in a casual atmosphere. Enjoy grilled grouper, crawfish salad, conch plate or a steak sandwich with sautéed mushrooms and onions. Other dishes include lamb chops, New York strip steak, fried shrimp and Cornish hen. Sandwiches are also available.

Live music keeps the action moving on Wednesday and Friday, and the happy hour packs the bar from 5 to 6:30 p.m. every night.

◆ **TIP**

If you're coming in by boat, you can radio in on VHF Channel 16 for reservations.

MAVIS COUNTRY RESTAURANT
Don McKay Boulevard
Marsh Harbour
☎ 242/367-2002 or 242/367-2050
Inexpensive
Dress code: casual
Reservations: not required

Located just south of the traffic light in downtown Marsh Harbour, this charming little eatery offers a real taste of Bahamian and Jamaican food, with good service and good prices to match. Vegetarian dishes, burgers and sandwiches are on the menu too. You'll probably have the chance to meet the owner and cook, Mavis Reckley, and be served by one of her two daughters.

Mavis' will pre-pare meals to take away.

On the menu you'll find such items as native grouper or snapper; chicken (steamed, barbecued, fried or baked); barbecued ribs; stewed beef; lamb chops; curried goat; curried chicken; ackee and saltfish; jerk chicken; and steamed oxtail.

NIPPERS BAR AND GRILL
Great Guana Cay
☎ 242/365-5143
Moderate
Dress code: casual
Reservations: suggested

This restaurant is perched on the edge of a bluff and offers a wonderful view of the world's third-largest barrier reef. Open for lunch and dinner, Nippers serves local specialties as well as a pig roast on Sundays.

THE PALMS BEACH CLUB AND BAR
Green Turtle Cay
☎ 242/365-4247
Inexpensive
Dress code: casual
Reservations: not required

This casual eatery is part of Bluff House and offers a relaxed setting for lunch. Local specialties are especially wonderful, particularly the cracked conch.

The Abacos

THE SPINNAKER RESTAURANT
Treasure Cay
☎ 242/365-8469
Inexpensive to Moderate
Dress code: casual
Reservations: suggested

Breakfast, lunch and dinner are served at this eatery. Lunch offerings include Bahamian fried fish, a spicy concoction, while evening guests can select from more gourmet items such as duck à l'orange and filet mignon Béarnaise. The Spinnaker Restaurant is, like the island itself, casual and fun.

Sunup to Sundown

Island Sightseeing

ALBERT LOWE MUSEUM
Main Street, Marsh Harbour
☎ 343/365-4094
Hours: weekdays; call for hours
Admission: donation

This museum showcases the history of the Abacos and its shipbuilding traditions. The museum was founded by Alton Lowe in memory of his father, a well-known ship model craftsman.

PEOPLE-TO-PEOPLE PROGRAM
☎ 242/326-5371, 242/328-7810, 242/356-0435-8, fax 242/356-0434

For more information about this cultural program, see page 89.

WYANNIE MALONE HISTORICAL MUSEUM
Hope Town, Elbow Cay
☎ 242/366-0033
Hours: Sunday to Friday, 11-3, Saturday, 10:30-2:30
Admission: small fee

This small museum is filled with the rich history of this island. It's not worth a special trip for the casual visitor, but those interested in history should try to visit here.

Golf

TREASURE CAY GOLF COURSE
☎ 800/327-1584 or 242/365-8578

An 18-hole golf course designed by Dick Wilson is located a half-mile from Treasure Cay Resort and Marina. The course is 72 par, 6,985 yards and is perfect for devoted golfers who want to take a break from the crowds. You don't need a tee time here – just grab the clubs and go!

Scuba Diving & Snorkeling

The **Coral Gardens** are located outside of Green Turtle Cay. A popular wreck dive is the ***Adirondack***, a wooden ship sunk during the Civil War.

Several dive operators offer scuba diving and snorkeling excursions to these and other sites. Check with **Dive Abaco** in Marsh Harbour for all types of tours ranging from snorkel trips to night, shark and wreck dives. ☎ 800/247-5338 or 242/247-5338.

Turtles

Green Turtle Cay is home to, quite predict-
ably, green turtles. These are bred on farms
as a food source and you'll find turtle soup
and stew on several local menus. You'll also
find products made from turtle shells in
some local stores. Note, however, that im-
portation of these turtle products to the US
is illegal (even for international passengers
in transit through the US). If you purchase
any of these goods, they will be confiscated
by US Customs.

Bicycling

Abaco's quiet, relaxed atmosphere makes this a good
place for bicyclists. You'll find bikes for rent at these
shops; rates run about $5 per day. Motocycles are
also available at Rental Wheels Abaco for about $20
per day.

The Bike Shop, Elbow Cay, ☎ 242/366-0262

R&L Rent-a-Ride, Marsh Harbour, ☎ 242/367- 2744

Rental Wheels Abaco, ☎ 242/367-4643

Shop Till You Drop

ABACO GIFTS AND SUNSET SOUVENIRS
Marsh Harbour
☎ 242/367-2658

This shop sells items ranging from t-shirts to caps
and Cuban cigars.

SOLOMON'S MINES

Treasure Cay, ☎ 242/365-8132
Marsh Harbour, ☎ 242/367-3191
www.solomons-mines.com

This large shop sells plenty of high-priced items at good prices. Look for fine jewelry by Carrera y Carrera, crystal by Lalique and Baccarat, china by Lladro, Versace accessories and perfume by Chanel.

In the market for a fine watch? Breitling, Omega, Rado, Tag Heuer, Gucci, Raymond Weil watches are sold at this extensive shop.

Nightlife

Cinema

RND CINEMAS
Seventeen Shopping Plaza
Marsh Harbour, ☎ 242/367-4383
This multiplex has three screens.

The Abacos A-Z

The Abacos

Banks

Barclay's
Marsh Harbour, ☎ 242/367-2152

CIBC
Elbow Cay, ☎ 242/366-0296
Marsh Harbour, ☎ 242/367-2166
Man-O-War Cay, ☎ 242/365-6098

Royal Bank Of Canada
Marsh Harbour, ☎ 242/367-2420

Scotia Bank
Marsh Harbour, ☎ 242/367-2142

Grocery Stores

Abaco Market
Marsh Harbour, ☎ 242/367-2044

Bahamas Family Market
Marsh Harbour, ☎ 242/367-3714

Golden Harvest
Marsh Harbour, ☎ 242/367-2310

Guana Harbour Grocery
Great Guana Cay, ☎ 242/365-5067

Lowe's Food Store
Green Turtle Cay, ☎ 242/365-4243

Sid's Food Store
Green Turtle Cay, ☎ 242/365-4055

Emergency Phone Numbers

Emergencies . . . . ☎ 911
Hospital (Nassau) . ☎ 322-2861 or 322-8411
Ambulance . . . . ☎ 322-2221
Med Evac . . . . ☎ 322-2881
Air Ambulance . . . . ☎ 327-7077
Fire . . . . ☎ 911
Police . . . . ☎ 911

Andros

If you've flown from Miami to the Caribbean, you probably flew over Andros. This giant island spans 2,300 square miles and is one of the largest tracts of unexplored land in the hemisphere.

Andros is easy to spot from the air because it splinters like a waterlogged chunk of wood floating in the sea. The island is home to many lakes and inlets. Snorkelers and scuba divers find some of the best activity in the area here, with the third-largest barrier island in the world just offshore. "Andros may be one of our best kept secrets," says the Director General of the Ministry of Tourism. "With its peaceful villages and spectacular, unspoiled scenery, it's the perfect destination for those who really want to get away from it all. Yet it's quick and easy to reach."

Andros is a favorite destination for scuba diving.

Chickcharnies & Luscas

Andros is the home of the legendary Chickcharnies. These three-toed, red-eyed elves sport beards and feathers and supposedly live deep in the interior. The tale of these impish beasts has thrived on this island for generations, scaring young children and explaining away odd occurrences.

The Chickcharnies are not alone in Andros, however. This island is also home to the Luscas, said to resemble an octopus. These evil spirits are said to live in dark blue holes in the sea. Whenever their domain is threatened, the Luscas drag men and their boats to a watery death.

Andros

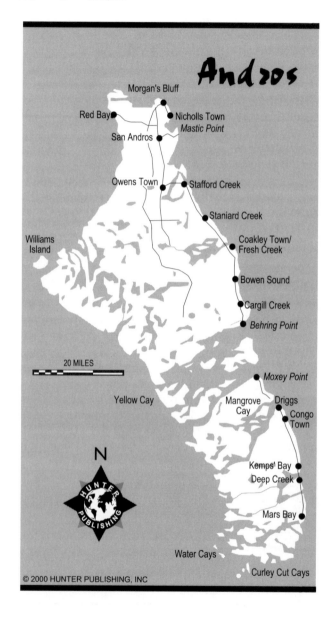

Andros

Morgan's Bluff

Red Bay

Nicholls Town

Mastic Point

San Andros

Owens Town

Stafford Creek

Staniard Creek

Williams
Island

Coakley Town/
Fresh Creek

Bowen Sound

Cargill Creek

Behring Point

20 MILES

Moxey Point

Yellow Cay

Mangrove
Cay

Driggs

Congo
Town

N

Kemps' Bay

Deep Creek

Mars Bay

Water Cays

© 2000 HUNTER PUBLISHING, INC

Curley Cut Cays

Best Places to Stay

See page 5 for price chart.

ANDROS ISLAND BONEFISHING CLUB
Cargill Creek
☎ 242/368-5167, fax 242/368-5235
Reservations: ☎ 800/688-4752
Moderate

This small hotel is, as the name suggests, a favorite with those looking for a few days of bonefishing. Guides are available for a day of fishing on the flats and the hotel even has a fly-tying table. The hotel has 12 rooms and a good restaurant.

ANDROS LIGHTHOUSE YACHT CLUB AND MARINA
Fresh Creek
☎ 242/368-2305, fax 242/368-2300
Reservations: ☎ 800/688-4752
Moderate

The 12 guest rooms here are located alongside an 18-slip marina. The rooms are just as you would imagine at a casual island resort: cool tile floors, light decor and plenty of sunshine. All rooms have a television and air conditioning; there's also a fresh-water pool here.

EMERALD PALMS BY-THE-SEA
Driggs Hill, South Andros
☎ 242/368-2661, fax 242/368-2667
Reservations: ☎ 800/688-4752
Moderate

This beachside option is just steps from the water and the nearby coral reef. All guest rooms feature air conditioning, ceiling fans, refrigerator and tele-visions.

Andros

SMALL HOPE BAY LODGE
Fresh Creek
☎ 242/368-2013 or 954/927-7096, fax 242/368-2015
Reservations: ☎ 800/223-6961
E-mail: shbmkt@smallhope.com
www.SmallHope.com
Moderate

Non-guests can visit Small Hope Bay to enjoy a meal at the restaurant.

A favorite with scuba divers, this lodge holds the title as one of the oldest hotels in the Bahamas, dating back to 1960. Guests can select from 20 one- and two-bedroom cottages on the beach, each decorated in a local style and built of native coral and rocks. The all-inclusive rate here covers all meals and drinks, airport transfers and use of snorkeling equipment, bicycles, sailboats, kayaks and windsurfers. Dive packages are available with three dives a day.

TRANQUILITY HILL BONEFISH LODGE
Behring Point
☎ 242/368-4132, fax 242/368-4132
Reservations: ☎ 800/688-4752
E-mail: tranquility@batelnet.bs
Moderate

Anglers consider this resort a favorite destination thanks to the on-site fishing guides and 16-foot skiffs. Guides specialize in bonefishing, although shark and deep-sea fishing excursions can also be arranged.

Best Places to Eat

See page 6 for price chart.

ANDROS ISLAND BONEFISHING CLUB
Cargill Creek
☎ 242/368-5167
Moderate
Dress code: casual
Reservations: suggested

Bring your fish tales to share at the Bonefishing Club!

Bahamian fare is the order of the day at this restaurant, starting with Bahamian pancakes for breakfast and continuing to dishes such as baked lobster, grouper, and peas 'n rice for lunch and dinner.

SMALL HOPE BAY LODGE
Fresh Creek
☎ 242/368-2013
Moderate
Dress code: casually elegant
Reservations: suggested

Small Hope Bay Lodge offers a salad bar and dessert bar at dinner.

This restaurant serves dishes using local produce, starting with an American-style breakfast and continuing with a lunch buffet. Local seafood, including lobster and conch, are the specialties for the evening meal.

Andros

Sunup to Sundown

Scuba Diving

As home of the largest reef in the Western Hemisphere and the third-largest in the world, it's no surprise that this is a favorite destination with scuba divers. Waters start shallow on the reef, just six to 15 feet, but drop to inky black depths at the **Tongue of the Ocean**, a deepwater trench.

The waters surrounding these islands are also dotted with shipwrecks. The *Lady Gloria*, a mailboat sunk off Morgan's Bluff, and the *Potomac,* a steel-hulled barge that now is filled with grouper, parrot fish and barracuda, are two favorite sites.

SMALL HOPE BAY LODGE
☎ 800/223-6961, 242/368-2014
www.smallhope.com

This dive facility offers daily dives ranging from a two-tank morning dive to a one-tank afternoon dive. Night dives are offered twice-weekly if there is sufficient interest. Guests at the lodge have the option of booking a dive package.

Andros A-Z

Banks

Bank Of The Bahamas
Kemp's Bay, ☎ 242/369-1787
Mangrove Cay, ☎ 242/369-0502

Emergency Phone Numbers

Emergencies	☎ 911
Hospital (Nassau)	☎ 322-2861 or 322-8411
Ambulance	☎ 322-2221
Med Evac	☎ 322-2881
Air Ambulance	☎ 327-7077
Fire	☎ 911
Police	☎ 911

Grocery Store

Ferguson Food Store
Kemp's Bay
☎ 242/369-1625

Pharmacies

Johnson Bay
Community Drug Store
Johnson Bay
☎ 242/369-4563

The Berry Islands

Haven't heard of the Berry Islands? You're probably not alone. This family of islands is largely uninhabited. Over 30 islands and cays (many privately owned) make up the chain, which is sprinkled 150 miles east of Miami and 35 miles north of Nassau.

Anglers love the Berry Islands!

These quiet islands, however, are well known in gamefishing circles. Serious anglers come to the islands, just like nearby Bimini, to try their luck at marlin, sailfish or mackerel.

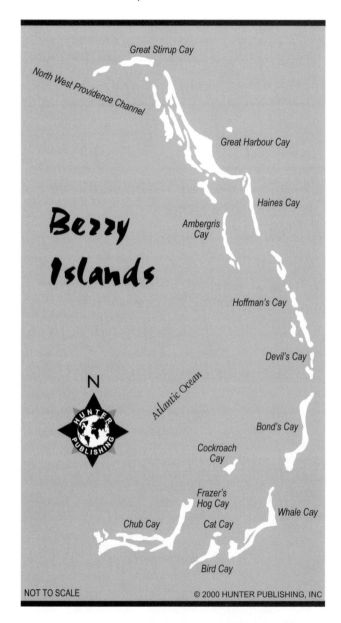

Great Stirrup Cay

North West Providence Channel

Great Harbour Cay

Haines Cay

Berry

Ambergris
Cay

Islands

Hoffman's Cay

Devil's Cay

N

Atlantic Ocean

Bond's Cay

Cockroach
Cay

Frazer's
Hog Cay

Whale Cay

Chub Cay

Cat Cay

Bird Cay

NOT TO SCALE

© 2000 HUNTER PUBLISHING, INC

Best Places to Stay

See page 5 for price chart.

GREAT HARBOUR CAY
YACHT CLUB AND MARINA
Great Harbour Cay
☎ 242/367-8838, fax 242/367-8115
Reservations: ☎ 800/343-7256
Moderate to Expensive

Great Harbour Cay is a private island and home to these villas and two-bedroom townhouses. Rooms include air conditioning, full kitchens and linens. An 80-slip marina is located here as well.

All accommodations have maid service at Great Harbour Cay.

CHUB CAY
One mile from Chub Cay Airport
☎ 242/325-1490, fax 242/322-5199
Moderate to Expensive

This 16-room resort has air conditioning in all its rooms and villas. All accommodations have a phone, cable TV, coffee-maker, refrigerator and private bath. This is a popular option with active travelers, offering scuba diving, deep-sea fishing, bonefishing, tennis courts and bike rentals. It has a restaurant, marina, laundry room, two pools and a bar.

Best Places to Eat

See page 6 for price chart.

THE BEACH CLUB
Great Harbour Cay
☎ 242/367-8838
Inexpensive
Dress code: casual
Reservations: not required

Berry Islands

This restaurant serves breakfast and lunch as well as cocktails until 6 p.m. Located at Great Harbour Cay Yacht Club, this club is a favorite place for yachties to gather and share stories.

TAMBOO DINNER CLUB
Great Harbour Cay
☎ 242/367-8838
Moderate
Dress code: casually elegant
Reservations: required

This restaurant is open for dinner only and serves a variety of continental and Bahamian dishes. It sits at the end of the marina and is a great place to come at the end of the day for a tasty meal.

Sunup to Sundown

Scuba Diving

Like Andros, the Berry Islands are located just off the **Tongue of the Ocean**, a 6,000-foot-deep trench that offers scuba divers plenty of reef and wall dives. One of the top dive sites is **Mamma Rhoda Rock**. This 16-foot dive along the coral reef brings enthusiasts face to face with many crawfish and moray eels. Hoffman Cay's **blue hole**, over 600 feet deep, is another popular site.

Scuba guides and equipment rental are avialable through **Club Bay Resort**, ☎ 242/325-1490.

The Bimini Islands

Just 50 miles east of Miami lie the Biminis, a chain of islands and cays closer than any others to the US. You often hear "Bimini" as a single destination, but travelers should set their course for North Bimini, South Bimini, or one of the other many cays such as Gun Cay, Ocean Cay or the ritzy private island of Cat Cay.

The Biminis are popular with anglers, as well as those looking for a quick getaway

If you've heard of the Biminis, it is probably due to Ernest Hemingway, undoubtedly the most famous Bimini booster. The writer came to these islands to pen *Islands in the Stream* and *To Have and Have Not* as well as to fish, swap fish tales, and down a few cold ones at The Compleat Angler bar.

Today Ernest's seat at the bar has been taken over by any number of other gamefishermen, who come from around the globe to test their skills in what is often called the "Gamefishing Capital of the World." Records have been set here for trophy sailfish, tuna and wahoo.

The largest destination in this chain is **North Bimini**, which measures 7½ miles long. The island's main community is called Alice Town.

Bimini Legends & Mysteries

The Biminis have a rich history that continues to interest many people, especially those with an eye for mystery. These islands are home to four mystical sites:

The Lost City of Atlantis

When you fly over the Bimini Islands, the Bimini Road is easy to see from the air.

Yes, rumor has it that the Lost City of Atlantis just might have been found. Researchers began the task of studying large stones that appear to be part of an underground road, which would date this region to 10,000 B.C.

Sand Mounds

Researchers are also puzzled by large sand mounds in the shape of a shark, cat and a seahorse that lie on the sea floor near North Bimini. These are so huge their shapes can be seen only from the air. Just so you don't think that this was the work of some trickster, know that the mounds appear on early maps of the island – maps drawn at a time when there was no air travel.

The Fountain of Youth

Ponce DeLeon came to the Biminis in 1513 in search of the elusive fountain. Supposedly, the explorer was given directions by the local Indians and told to search for it in a place called BeeMeeNee.

The Healing Hole

A labyrinth of narrow tunnels lies north of the Biminis. One of these tunnels is connected to a creek that is called The Healing Hole. At high tide, the tunnels fill with water and empty into the creek. The waters, which are high in mineral content, are said to have mystical healing powers.

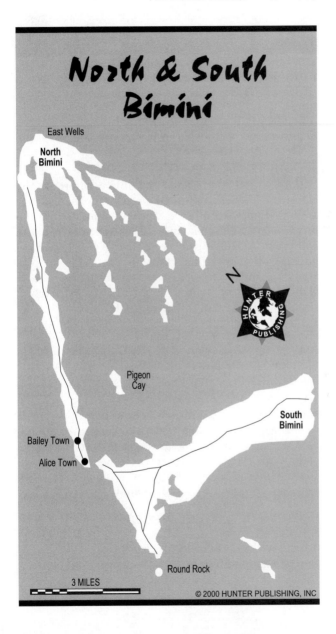

Best Places to Stay

BIMINI BIG GAME FISHING CLUB AND HOTEL
Alice Town
☎ 242/347-3391, fax 242/347-3392
Reservations: ☎ 800/737-1007
Moderate to Expensive
www.bimini-big-game-club.com

Probably the best known accommodation in the Biminis, this hotel offers 49 guest rooms and plenty of fishing opportunities as well as scuba diving. Deluxe rooms, cottages and a penthouse suite are available. All have private patios. The rooms have an island feel and comfortable atmosphere. Air conditioning and satellite TV are standard. The hotel is also home to the Gulfstream Restaurant, Gulfstream Bar and the Barefoot Bar.

BIMINI BLUE WATER RESORT
Alice Town
☎ 242/347-3066, fax 242/347-3293
Inexpensive to Moderate

The Blue Water Resort is located alongside a marina with full boating facilities. Guests can select from rooms with two double beds, suites with two bedrooms and a sitting room, and the three-bedroom cottage with kitchen. The resort is home to The Anchorage Restaurant. All rooms have a television, mini-refrigerator and a bathroom with shower.

COMPLEAT ANGLER HOTEL

The Compleat Angler is now part of the Blue Water Resort (above).

Alice Town
☎ 242/347-3122, fax 242/347-3293
Inexpensive to Moderate

Hemingway buffs might enjoy a stay at this small, 12-room hotel where the literary giant once rested.

Today, he is remembered with photos that are displayed in the public areas. The writer stayed in the Marlin Cottage; it has a fireplace and kitchen.

This is not a luxurious place, but the rooms are simply yet comfortable. Much of the activity focuses on the bar, a good place to chat with anglers.

Best Places to Eat

THE ANCHORAGE
Bimini Blue Water Resort
Alice Town
☎ 242/347-3066
Moderate
Dress code: casual
Reservations: suggested

This restaurant, styled like a Cape Cod house, is open for lunch and dinner. It's nothing fancy – we're talking Formica here – but serves good local food and fresh fish.

THE COMPLEAT ANGLER
Alice Town
☎ 242/347-3122
Inexpensive
Dress code: casual
Reservations: not required

It's a watering hole only (no food), but a stop by this famous Bimini bar is a must. Papa Hemingway called this place home on more than one occasion and today it remembers its most famous patron with the Ernest Hemingway Museum, a collection of paintings and pictures.

Hemingway buffs must make a stop at The Compleat Angler!

END OF THE WORLD BAR
Alice Town
Inexpensive
Dress code: casual
Reservations: not required

End Of The World Bar has a sand and sawdust floor.

This supercasual bar had its 15 minutes of fame when the late Congressman Adam Clayton Powell used to hang out here as something of a local hero. Drop by for a rum punch and bring along something to add to the collection of clothing, business cards, caps and more that fill every available inch of wall space.

GULFSTREAM BAR
Bimini Big Game Fishing Club and Hotel
Alice Town
☎ 242/347-3391
Inexpensive
Dress code: casual
Reservations: not required
www.bimini-big-game-club.com

Gulfstream is another good spot to swap your fishy tales!

This bar opens after the hotel's other drinking hole (Barefoot Bar) closes and stays open late. A favorite stop not only for their often-praised rum punch but also just to hang out and enjoy the relaxed atmosphere.

When you're ready to eat, drop in at the Gulfstream Restaurant (see below).

GULFSTREAM RESTAURANT
Bimini Big Game Fishing Club and Hotel
Alice Town
☎ 242/347-3391
Moderate to Expensive
Dress code: casually elegant
Reservations: recommended
www.bimini-big-game-club.com

This breakfast and dinner restaurant serves seafood, chicken, steaks and more. It also has an extensive wine list.

The restaurant is famous for its Bahamian cuisine and fresh seafood. American dishes are also offered.

Sunup to Sundown

Island Sightseeing

THE COMPLEAT ANGLER HOTEL
Alice Town
☎ 242/347-3122
Hours: 7 a.m.-midnight

Drop by for a look at the Hemingway memorabilia and even some of his writings. While it's not worth a special trip to Bimini, we do recommend you stop by if you're on the island. Hemingway buffs love it!

FOUNTAIN OF YOUTH
South Bimini

Hire a local guide or rent a car to find this pool near the airport (there is a marker). This site is allegedly the Fountain of Youth that Ponce DeLeon was searching for in 1513 (see page 148 for full details).

PEOPLE-TO-PEOPLE PROGRAM
☎ 242/326-5371, 242/328-7810, 242/356-0435-8, fax 242/356-0434

For more details on this unique cultural program, see page 89.

Scuba Diving

The mysterious **Bimini Wall,** a site that some say was either a road or part of the Lost City of Atlantis, is a favorite scuba destination.

If you're looking for a wreck dive, head out to the wreck of the ***Sapora***, a cement-hulled ship built as a troop carrier in WWI. The ship (which moved from war to combating rum running) ran aground during a hurricane and soon began a new career as a dive site and a fish home. The wreck sits in very shallow waters (about 15 feet) and part of it is visible above the water.

The Sapora *is a good snorkel site and a good place for beginner divers.*

Scuba diving is available through **Bimini Undersea Adventures** (☎ 242/347-3089).

Sportfishing

Numerous operators will take serious anglers out for a half- or full-day of big game fishing for bluefin tuna, tarpon, dolphin, amberjack, white and blue marlin, swordfish, barracuda, grouper and shark.

Several marinas in Alice Town offer charter fishing cruises and guides to show you the best fishing spots; check with the marina offices or call the **Bahamas Out Islands Promotion Board** (☎ 800/688-4752 or 242/352-8044).

The Bimini Islands A-Z

Banks

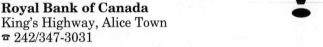

Royal Bank of Canada
King's Highway, Alice Town
☎ 242/347-3031

Grocery Store

Jontra's Grocery
Alice Town
☎ 242/347-3401

Cat Island

Cat Island is home of the highest peak in the Bahamas – all 206 feet of it! Mount Alvernia isn't exactly high enough to cause nosebleeds, but it does lend an interesting summit to this large island, the sixth-largest in the Bahamas.

Cat Island is 325 miles southeast of Miami.

Cat Island is a favorite diving destination.

> ◆ **TIP**
>
> Cat Island is not at all the same as private Cat Cay, located in the Biminis. Don't confuse the two!

Cat Island

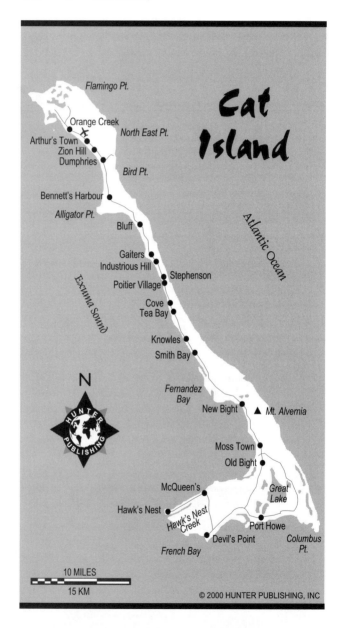

Cat Island

Flamingo Pt.

Orange Creek
Arthur's Town
Zion Hill
Dumphries

North East Pt.

Bird Pt.

Bennett's Harbour

Alligator Pt.

Bluff

Gaiters
Industrious Hill
Poitier Village
Stephenson

Cove
Tea Bay

Knowles

Smith Bay

Fernandez
Bay

New Bight ▲ Mt. Alvernia

Moss Town
Old Bight

McQueen's

Great
Lake

Hawk's Nest

Hawk's Nest
Creek

Port Howe

Devil's Point

French Bay

Columbus
Pt.

Atlantic Ocean

Exuma Sound

N

HUNTER
PUBLISHING

10 MILES

15 KM

© 2000 HUNTER PUBLISHING, INC

"Cat"

Two theories account for the island's name:

A) Wild cats that supposedly were descended from cats left by Spanish colonists, or

B) Captain Arthur Catt, a British sea captain (sometimes termed a pirate).

Best Places to Stay

GREENWOOD BEACH RESORT
Cat Island Dive Centre
Port Howe
☎/fax 242/342-3053
Reservations: ☎ 800/688-4752
Inexpensive
www.greenwoodbeachresort.com

A favorite with divers, this 20-room resort is located on eight miles of beach. All rooms have private baths. We recommend this resort for active travelers. Guests can borrow bikes and explore the island, take a snorkel tour or go scuba diving. The resort offers an excellent restaurant.

HAWK'S NEST RESORT AND MARINA
Hawk's Nest
☎/fax 242/357-7257
Reservations: ☎ 800/OUT-ISLAND
www.hawks-nest.com
Moderate to Expensive

Ten guest rooms offer quiet privacy at this hotel with its own airstrip. Rooms feature air conditioning, ceiling fans and private baths. Guests have access to a clubhouse, restaurant and beach. Rooms are beachfront, with ocean view, air conditioning, private patio and full bath.

Best Places to Eat

GREENWOOD BEACH RESORT
☎ 242/342-3053
Moderate
Dress code: casual
Reservations: suggested

Dine outdoors at this beachside restaurant that serves Bahamian and international cuisine. The roofed terrace is a great place to take a break from the sun for lunch.

HAWK'S NEST RESORT
☎ 242/357-7257
Inexpensive to Moderate
Dress code: casually elegant
Reservations: required

Located near the marina, this restaurant serves Bahamian cuisine as well as American dishes. Open for breakfast, lunch and dinner. The restaurant, with its stone walls and small tables, has an intimate feel.

Sunup to Sundown

Island Sightseeing

COLUMBUS POINT

This Arawak cave is near where locals believe Christopher Columbus first made landfall in the New World. Located on the southeast point of the island.

THE HERMITAGE AT MT. ALVERNIA
New Bight

A replica of a European hermitage, this meditation spot was built by Father Jerome in the 1940s using limestone from Mt. Alvernia, the island's highest point. It will take about 15 minutes to hike to the top of the hill, and you'll be rewarded with a view of the island that can't be beat! The structure is located east of the town of New Bight.

Cat Island

Cat Island A-Z

Emergency Phone Numbers

```
Emergencies . . . . . . . . . . . . . . ☎ 911
Hospital (Nassau) . ☎ 322-2861 or 322-8411
Ambulance . . . . . . . . . . . . ☎ 322-2221
Med Evac. . . . . . . . . . . . . ☎ 322-2881
Air Ambulance . . . . . . . . . . ☎ 327-7077
Fire . . . . . . . . . . . . . . . . . . ☎ 911
Police . . . . . . . . . . . . . . . . . ☎ 911
```

Crooked Island & Acklins Island

Crooked and Acklins Islands almost look like one landmass, but are separated by the Crooked Island Passage. These islands were once the home of Loyalists who left America after the Revolution and came to settle on these islands perched on shallow waters.

The waters around Crooked & Acklins Islands are especially attractive to anglers & scuba divers.

Crooked Island was called "Isabella" by Columbus in honor of his queen. Today, this quiet place 240 miles from Nassau is home to only 700 residents. Visitors here find many beautiful beaches.

Acklins Island is separated from Crooked Island by a one-mile wide stretch of water. If you've got a bad case of the "been there, done that's," Acklins may be a good destination for you. It is a rare destination for anyone, although here you'll find good scuba diving, fishing and swimming.

Best Place to Stay

PITTSTOWN POINT LANDING
Landrail Point
☎ 242/344-2507, fax 242/344-2507
Reservations: ☎ 800/PLACE2B
www.pittstown.com
Inexpensive

No plane? No problem. You can also arrive here via a scheduled BahamasAir flight.

On the northwest shore of Crooked Island, this 12-room property is very popular with private pilots because of its landing strip.

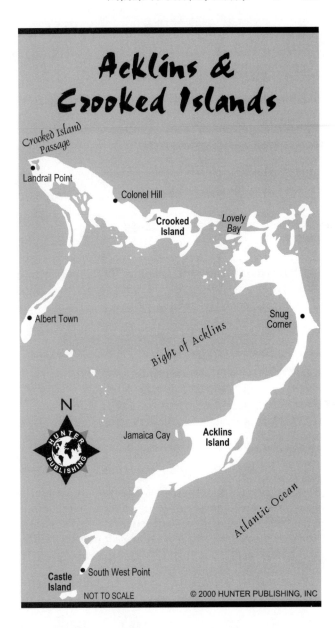

Acklins &
Crooked Islands

Crooked Island
Passage

Landrail Point

Colonel Hill

Crooked
Island

Lovely
Bay

Albert Town

Snug
Corner

Bight of Acklins

N

Jamaica Cay

Acklins
Island

Atlantic Ocean

Castle
Island

South West Point

NOT TO SCALE

© 2000 HUNTER PUBLISHING, INC

Acklins & Crooked Islands

Rooms here hug the beach; facilities and activities include scuba diving (you'll find plenty of action just offshore), bonefishing, deep-sea fishing, shuffleboard and volleyball.

The hotel's dining room (Ozzie's Café) serves breakfast, lunch and dinner. Guests can also have a picnic lunch prepared with a day's notice.

Eleuthera & Harbour Island

Eleuthera is the kind of place that sneaks into your thoughts when you're stuck in the office fantasizing about an island getaway.

★ DID YOU KNOW?

In Greek, Eleuthera means "Freedom." It's a favorite retreat for those seeking a few days of freedom from hectic schedules.

Eleuthera is popular with anglers and scuba divers.

To the first English settlers, Eleutera meant religious freedom. The Eleutheran Adventurers came to this land because it resembled English farmland. Located 60 miles east of Nassau, Eleuthera is hilly and fertile, and it is the most developed of any of the Bahamian Out Islands.

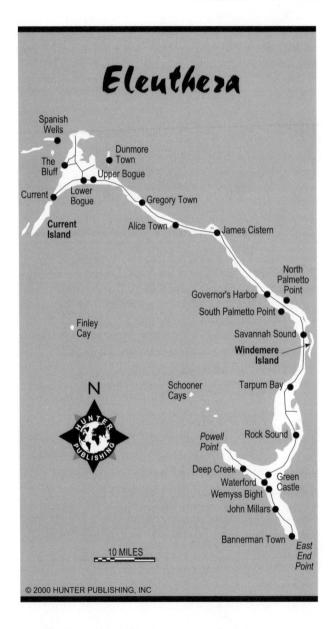

© 2000 HUNTER PUBLISHING, INC

Ask a local resident about his island, however, and he'll call it Cigatoo, the local name for this 200-square-mile piece of land. Whatever you call it, you'll find plenty of fun, including numerous dive sites, snorkeling and bonefishing.

Just two miles off Eleuthera's northern coast lies **Harbour Island**, connected to its larger cousin by ferry service. This three-mile-long island is just half a mile wide, but it is the home of several attractions.

Much of the activity takes place in **Dunmore Town**, where the streets are lined with clapboard houses, most with beautiful gardens.

★ DID YOU KNOW?

Locals call Harbour Island "Briland," and local residents are known as Brilanders.

Eleuthera Style

- ◎ Golf carts are one of the most popular means of transportation on this tiny island.

- ◎ The island was used by rum runners during Prohibition.

- ◎ Architecture here is New England-style.

- ◎ Visitors to the island are often called "seaweed" because they "wash up on the beach."

Best Places to Stay

CLUB MED ELEUTHERA

Governor's Harbour
☎ 242/332-2270, fax 242/332-2855
Reservations: ☎ 800/CLUB MED
www.clubmed.com
Moderate

This all-inclusive is a favorite with families who love the special programs for children two years and older. Petit, Mini and Kids Clubs offer plenty of activity for young vacationers, and adults find lots of action as well: bocce ball, circus workshops, golf, fishing, sailing, scuba diving, soccer, softball, tennis and more. Three restaurants offer plenty of dining options.

> ◆ **NOTE**
>
> At press time, Club Med Eleuthera was closed because of damage from Hurricane Floyd in September 1999. Look for the property to reopen in July 2000.

CORAL SANDS HOTEL AND RESORT

Dunmore Town, Harbour Island
☎ 242/333-2350, fax 242/333-2368
Reservations: ☎ 800/468-2799
www.coralsands.com
E-mail: Reservations@coralsands.com
Moderate to Deluxe

Do you like country inns? If so, then this little property on the beach may be just the place for you. The 23-room resort is reached by taxi and ferry and is a

Eleuthera

real getaway. Some rooms have beachview private balconies, kitchens and refrigerators. Guest amenities include fishing, sailing, snorkeling, swimming, tennis and a dining room that offers fine cuisine. The resort has a Cordon Bleu-certified chef at its new Poseidon restaurant.

PINK SANDS
Harbour Island
☎ 242/333-2030, fax 242/333-2060
Reservations: ☎ 800/OUTPOST
www.islandoutpost.com
Expensive to Deluxe

This 29-room resort offers 21 one-bedroom cottages and four two-bedroom cottages with a living room area. Located on, yes, a pink sand beach, the resort boasts a laid-back atmosphere. It has a freshwater pool, three tennis courts (one lit for night play), exercise studio, Club House, library and more. The resort can arrange for golf cart and bicycle rentals as well.

The two restaurants at Pink Sands offer local dishes with a gourmet flair. The Blue Bar serves lunch right on the beach while breakfast and dinner are in the main dining area.

Pink Sands is part of the popular Island Outpost chain of fine, small inns.

RAMORA BAY CLUB
Harbour Island
☎ 242/333-2325, fax 242/333-2500
Moderate

This 38-room hotel is on a hillside with a harbor view. Most rooms have a patio or balcony; some offer kitchens. Guest recreation includes scuba diving, windsurfing, sailing, tennis and beach access. A dining room serves breakfast, lunch and dinner.

Best Places to Eat

THE BLUE BAR
Pink Sands Resort
Harbour Island
☎ 242/333-2030
Moderate
Dress code: casual
Reservations: not required

This beach bar brings typical lunchtime fare up several notches with such dishes as Bahamian conch chowder spiked with dark rum, conch and cilantro fritters with Pickapeppa mayo, and West Indian chicken spring rolls with tandoori-pineapple dip. The atmosphere is casual, the perfect place to go after a few hours on the beach.

PINK SANDS MAIN DINING ROOM
Pink Sands
Harbour Island
☎ 242/333-2030
Moderate to Expensive
Dress code: casually elegant
Reservations: recommended

Breakfast and dinner are served at this al fresco eatery filled with teak furniture that echoes the tropical surroundings. Diners enjoy private candlelit tables and a romantic atmosphere in this intimate restaurant.

Dinner always features a pre-set menu with a four-course meal including: appetizer, soup or salad, entrée, dessert and coffee or tea. Favorite appetizers include tuna and sweet potato cakes with cilantro and soya dressing; Thai shrimp sautéed in sesame seed oil and lemongrass, and Bahamian sushi roll with mango, cucumber and conch. Dinner entrées

Pink Sands guests can order a meal delivered to the room. include such choices as blackened grouper; cornmeal-dusted Cornish hen served on spinach with a tamarind-honey vinaigrette; or local fresh lobster tail with cilantro and sesame butter. Dinner is served from 7 p.m. to 9 p.m.

POSEIDON RESTAURANT
Coral Sands Resort
☎ 242/333-2350
Moderate to Expensive
Dress code: casually elegant
Reservations: recommended

This new restaurant features both European as well as Bahamian cuisine. Dishes are flavored with herbs straight from the resort's garden, all prepared by the Cordon Bleu-trained chef Susan Neff. You'll find plenty of fresh catch on the menu – everything from conch to lobster to grouper.

Sunup to Sundown

Island Sightseeing

PEOPLE-TO-PEOPLE PROGRAM
☎ 242/326-5371, 242/328-7810,
☎ 242/356-0435-8, fax 242/356-0434

To learn more about the People-To-People program, see page 89.

Scuba Diving

Eleuthera is home to one of the most unusual dive sites in the region: **Train Wreck**. Lying in just 15 feet of water off the island's north end, this site contains the remains of a loco-

tive and several railroad cars that sank off a barge.
(Why, you ask, were railroad cars being transported
off Eleuthera? The island was used as a port by the
US Confederate states during the Civil War when
southern ports were blocked.)

VALENTINE'S DIVE CENTER
PO Box 1
Harbour Island
☎/fax 242/333-2309

This full-service shop offers three to four dives daily
and all levels of instruction.

Golf

COTTON BAY CLUB GOLF COURSE
Rock Sound, ☎ 800/334-3523

Designed by Robert Trent Jones, this 18-hole course
has 13 water hazards.

Eleuthera A-Z

Banks

Bank of Nova Scotia
Bogue
☎ 242/335-1400

Barclays Bank
Rock Sound
☎ 242/334-2022

Royal Bank of Canada
Governor's Harbour
☎ 242/356-2856

Eleuthera

Grocery Stores

Sands Enterprises Store
Governor's Harbour
☎ 242/332-1651

Sands Enterprises Supermarket
Palmetto Point
☎ 242/332-1662

Thompson's Supermarket
Gregory Town
☎ 242/335-5009

Emergency Phone Numbers

Emergencies . . . . ☎ 911
Hospital (Nassau) . . ☎ 322-2861, 322-8411
Ambulance . . . . ☎ 322-2221
Med Evac. . . . . ☎ 322-2881
Air Ambulance. . . . . ☎ 327-7077
Fire . . . . ☎ 911
Police . . . . ☎ 911

The Exuma Islands

The Exumas are a long-time favorite with sailors.

The Exumas are a whole chain of islands and cays – over 350 of them, to be precise. Located right in the middle of the Bahamas island chain, they are a favorite destination for the sailing crowd.

Most of the activity takes place on Great Exuma in the community of **George Town**. Shoppers can visit the town's Straw Market. A far cry from the two-story version in Nassau, this local outdoor market is very relaxed.

The islands also offer good deep-sea fishing and diving. Staniel Cay's **Thunderball Grotto** was used in the filming of the James Bond movie *Thunderball*. Another good site is **Highborne Cay Wreck**, where snorkelers can see the wreck in just 40 feet of water.

Great & Little Exuma

Baraterre
Rolleville
Alexander
Steventon
Exuma Sound
N
Mount Thompson
Great Exuma
Moss Town
Georgetown
Forbes Hill
Hog Cay
Rolletown
William's Town
Little Exuma
Hog Cay
10 MILES
© 2000 HUNTER PUBLISHING, INC

Best Places to Stay

CLUB PEACE AND PLENTY
George Town
☎ 242/336-2551, fax 242/336-2093
Reservations: ☎ 800/525-2210
E-mail: pandp@peaceandplenty.com
www.peaceandplenty.com
Moderate

This 35-room waterside hotel offers air-conditioned accommodations with harborview balconies. You'll find plenty of action here: twice-weekly cocktail parties, a freshwater pool, and beach fun at the Stocking Island Beach Club, which has snorkeling, undersea caves for exploration and sailing.

> ### ★ DID YOU KNOW?
>
> HRH Prince Philip and HRM King Constantine of Greece have both been guests at Club Peace and Plenty.

HOTEL HIGGINS LANDING
Stocking Island
☎ 242/336-2460
Reservations: ☎ 800/688-4752
www.higginslanding.com
Expensive to Deluxe

Higgins was named the Best Eco-tourism Resort in the Bahamas by the Islands magazine.

If you're looking for a small, ecologically-friendly resort where you can really get away from it all, here's the place. Located on Stocking Island, this property took four years to construct so as to make sure its impact on the island was minimal. Today it offers five cottages, each furnished with antique furniture, including a queen-sized bed. All rooms have a private bath and a ceiling fan.

Hotel Higgins features a gourmet restaurant. When it's time to work off those meals, take a swim at Silver Palms Beach on one side or explore Turtle Lagoon on the other (which is also a favorite spot for bonefishing).

PEACE AND PLENTY BEACH INN
George Town
☎ 242/336-2250, fax 242/336-2253
Reservations: ☎ 800/525-2210
E-mail: pandp@peaceandplenty.com
www.peaceandplenty.com
Moderate

The Peace & Plenty Beach Inn runs a shuttle bus service into George Town.

This beachside hotel offers 16 guest rooms, each with air conditioning, ceiling fan and private balcony.

PEACE AND PLENTY BONEFISH LODGE
George Town
☎ 242/345-5555, fax 242/345-5556
Reservations: ☎ 800/525-2210
E-mail: ppand@peaceandplenty.com
www.peaceandplenty.com
Moderate

Not surprisingly, bonefishermen dominate the guest list at this eight-room property. The lodge is made-to-order for anglers, with a tackle and pro shop, fly-tying facilities and a sports art gallery on site.

The Bonefish Lodge is a great place for telling that fish tale!

STANIEL CAY YACHT CLUB
Staniel Cay
☎ 242/355-2024, fax 242/355-2044
Moderate

This waterfront property offers cottages for two to four people and a house that accommodates seven.

Guests have use of a marina, dive shop and Boston Whalers.

Best Places to Eat

CLUB PEACE AND PLENTY
☎ 242/336-2551
Inexpensive to Moderate
Dress code: casual
Reservations: optional

Start your evening at Club Peace & Plenty with a drink at the Reef Bar on the pool deck.

This eatery serves breakfast, lunch and dinner. It specializes in Bahamian food, but also serves American cuisine.

HOTEL HIGGINS LANDING
Stocking Island
☎ 800/688-4752, 242/336-2460
www.higginslanding.com
Moderate to Expensive
Dress code: casually elegant
Reservations: required

A gourmet menu featuring local seafood with a chef's special touches brings guests to this hotel restaurant. Dining is available indoors by candlelight or outdoors.

STANIEL CAY YACHT CLUB
Staniel Cay
☎ 242/355-2011
Moderate
Dress code: casual, casually elegant
Reservations: optional

The Yacht Club is a favorite with the boating crowd.

Yachties can pick up a boxed lunch or enjoy breakfast, lunch or dinner at this fun-loving club. The restaurant has fresh produce and meats flown in weekly and serves excellent local fish as well. Both Bahamian and continental fare are offered. Some of the best choices include lobster chowder, conch fritters and steaks.

Sunup to Sundown

PEOPLE-TO-PEOPLE PROGRAM
☎ 242/326-5371, 242/328-7810,
☎ 242/356-0435-8, fax 242/356-0434

To learn more about this cultural program, see page 89.

Scuba Diving

Diving is very good in the Exumas, thanks to the **Exuma Cays Land and Sea Park**, established by the National Trust. For more information about diving these waters, contact:

EXUMA DIVE CENTRE & WATERSPORTS
George Town
☎ 242/336-2390, fax 242/336-2391
www.bahamasvg.com/exumadive.html

This extensive dive center offers guided dive and snorkel trips, resort courses and instruction. Boat and scooter rentals are available.

The Exumas A-Z

Banks

Scotiabank
George Town
☎ 242/336-2651

Emergency Phone Numbers

```
Emergencies . . . . . . . . . . . . . . ☎ 911
Hospital (Nassau) . ☎ 322-2861 or 322-8411
Ambulance . . . . . . . . . . . . ☎ 322-2221
Med Evac. . . . . . . . . . . . . ☎ 322-2881
Air Ambulance . . . . . . . . . . ☎ 327-7077
Fire . . . . . . . . . . . . . . . . . ☎ 911
Police . . . . . . . . . . . . . . . . ☎ 911
```

Grand Bahama

Grand Bahama island is indeed a grand destination, starting with the city of **Freeport**. Stroll the streets of this bustling port and enjoy shopping for international and locally made goods.

Grand Bahamas is a favorite with shoppers and couples.

The **Port Lucaya Marketplace and Marina** offers shops selling perfumes, clothing and crafts, and usually has live music along its outdoor waterfront. You'll find goods from around the globe at the **International Bazaar**, and nearby the **Bahamas Arts and Crafts Market** sells locally made jewelry and baskets. The bazaar and market are adjacent to the **Resort at Bahamia** (formerly the Bahamas Princess Resort and Casino), where you can try your luck at table games or slot machines.

The city of Freeport/Lucaya was established just over 40 years ago as a tax-free base for trading nations of the west.

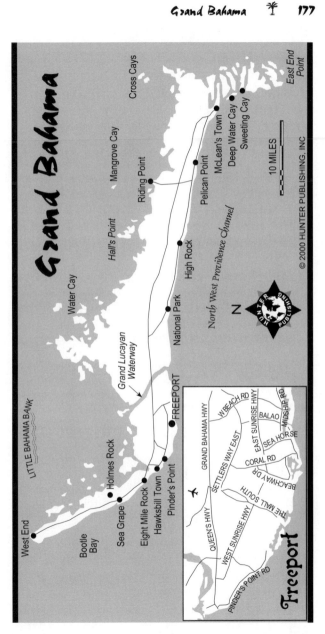

Grand Bahama

© 2000 HUNTER PUBLISHING, INC

Blue Holes

The seabed surrounding the Bahamas is dotted with "blue holes," deep, seemingly bottomless holes in the sea that are easily seen from the air.

These holes were formed when an underwater mountain range filled with glaciers during the Ice Age. As the glaciers grew, water levels dropped and the land peeked up from the sea. Once the glaciers melted, the seafloor became pocked with numerous holes and underground caverns.

Many of these underwater caverns have never been explored, although some, such as Gold Rock Blue Hole, have interested divers and geologists for some time.

Best Places to Stay

CLARION ATLANTIK BEACH HOTEL
Freeport
☎ 242/373-1444, fax 242/373-7481
Moderate

This 175-room resort is on Lucaya Beach and offers an array of watersports and beach fun, including parasailing. Some rooms feature kitchens, microwaves and refrigerators.

The Clarion is popular with family travelers. Its kids' program, Camp Lucaya, offers supervised games, activities and meals.

CLUB FORTUNA BEACH
Freeport
☎ 242/373-4000, fax 242/373-6181
Moderate

This all-inclusive resort, with over 200 guest rooms, has a Mediterranean feel. Visitors have a full range of activities from which to choose, including sailing, windsurfing, snorkeling, tennis and a golf driving range. There's also nightly entertainment.

◆ **NOTE**

Scuba diving and waterskiing aren't part of the all-inclusive package, but can be arranged.

THE LUCAYAN
Across from Port Lucaya
☎ 800/LUCAYAN
Moderate

The newest addition to Grand Bahama is this $250 million resort, boasting over 1,200 guest rooms, a full-service spa, two 18-hole championship golf courses, five tennis courts, 15 restaurants, a casino, three pools, and a 10,000-square-foot shopping complex. Families will appreciate the Kids Camp, while adults and children will like the Marine Educational Program created in conjunction with UNEXSO to teach more about the marine life of the area.

◆ **NOTE**

At press time, some phases of this new resort had yet to be opened. Check for an update.

Grand Bahama

PORT LUCAYA RESORT AND YACHT CLUB

Bell Channel Road
☎ 242/373-6618, fax 242/373-6652
Moderate

This 160-room resort is adjacent to the Port Lucaya Marketplace. Guests have beach access as well as a playground, marina, restaurant, pool and more.

RESORT AT BAHAMIA

Freeport
☎ 242/352-9661, fax 242/352-2542
Moderate to Deluxe

Guest rooms at this sprawling resort (formerly the Bahamas Princess Resort & Casino) include 400 rooms in the 10-story tower as well as 565 two- and three-story low-rise accommodations. All rooms have two double beds, cable TV, direct dial telephone, and a host of other comforts. The resort has a wide array of dining options, including Guanahani's, the Rib Room, Morgan's Bluff, and Crown Room (for more details on these establishments, see below).

Best Places to Eat

CROWN ROOM

Resort at Bahamia
Freeport
☎ 242/352-9661
Expensive
Dress code: dressy, jacket required
Reservations: required

This gourmet eatery serves continental cuisine in an elegant atmosphere. Decor includes mirrors, crystal chandeliers and muted lighting. We recommend the Crown Room to couples in search of a quiet, romantic atmosphere.

GUANAHANI'S
Resort at Bahamia
Freeport
☎ 242/352-9661
Moderate to Expensive
Dress code: casually elegant
Reservations: suggested

Overlooking the pool, this Bahamian-style restaurant boasts a tropical atmosphere complete with rattan chairs, verdant palms and ceiling fans.

Bahamian specialties fill the menu, including such delightful dishes as native grouper and barbecue spare ribs. Located in the tower at the Resort at Bahamia, the restaurant sports a nautical theme.

MORGAN'S BLUFF RESTAURANT
Resort at Bahamia
Freeport
☎ 242/352-9661
Moderate
Dress code: casually elegant
Reservations: suggested

This dinner-only restaurant serves Bahamian specialties such as conch chowder, conch salad, cracked conch, conch fritters and other seafood. A good option if you want to sample local dishes.

RIB ROOM
Resort at Bahamia
Freeport
☎ 242/352-9661
Expensive
Dress code: casually elegant or dressy
Reservations: suggested

This formal steakhouse serves seafood and steaks. The masculine atmosphere includes rough-hewn timber-beamed ceilings and red leather chairs. The place to come for an evening of quiet dining.

Sunup to Sundown

Island Sightseeing

BAHAMAS ARTS AND CRAFTS MARKET
Freeport
Hours: daily; open daytime hours
Admission: free

This market sells locally made jewelry and baskets. Located adjacent to the Resort at Bahamia. Like many craft markets, this one offers items of varying quality. We recommend it for inexpensive souvenirs. Expect to negotiate on prices.

GARDEN OF THE GROVES BOTANICAL GARDEN
Lucaya
Hours: afternoons; closed Mondays
Admission charged

This 12-acre botanical garden is home to over 10,000 varieties of flowers, trees and shrubs from around the world. Quiet, shaded paths wind through the gardens; you can take time, sit by a waterfall and hear the call of native birds.

INTERNATIONAL BAZAAR
Freeport
Hours: 10-6, Monday to Saturday
Admission: free

The atmosphere is global at this international bazaar. Narrow streets feature many types of architecture and shops showcasing merchandise from distant lands. Cuisines from around the world lend an exotic touch to this shopping district.

LUCAYAN NATIONAL PARK
Grand Bahama Highway
☎ 242/352-5738
Hours: daily; open daytime hours
Admission: free

This 40-acre park is filled with mangroves, pine and palm trees. You'll also find six miles of charted caves as well as a secluded beach, hiking trails and picnicking. The park is home to an enormous network of underwater caves too.

∕ WARNING

Dving in the underwater caves is prohibited without a permit from UNEXSO (☎ 242/373-1244, fax 242/373-8956). Even swimming in the caves is a no-no.

PEOPLE-TO-PEOPLE PROGRAM
☎ 242/352-8044, fax 242/352-2714
Hours: by arrangement
Admission: free

This unique program pairs vacationers with Bahamian volunteers. Before your visit, contact the Ministry of Tourism number above with an idea of what kind of experience you might like to have while on Grand Bahama Island. Want to go grocery shopping and prepare a local specialty with an island cook in a home kitchen? Want your family to spend the day with a local family enjoying sailing or beachcombing? Whatever your interest, the people at this office will try to match you with people who share your interests.

PORT LUCAYA MARKETPLACE
AND MARINA
Lucaya
Hours: 10-6, Monday to Saturday
Admission: free

Port Lucaya is a good place to visit on a rainy day.

Another favorite is the Port Lucaya Marketplace and Marina. Shops here offer perfumes, clothing and crafts. Live music along the outdoor waterfront usually keeps the atmosphere upbeat. As you'll find in other markets across the globe, the quality of items sold here can vary greatly. This is a fun stop, even if you don't buy a thing.

RAND MEMORIAL NATURE CENTRE
East Settler's Way, Freeport
☎ 242/352-5438
Hours: 9-4, Monday through Friday; 1-4 Saturday
Admission charged
www.bahamasnet.com/rand

The Rand Memorial Nature Centre is home to over 200 species of feathered friends and is a favorite stop with birders. You'll also find a replica of a Lucayan village.

UNEXSO'S THE DOLPHIN EXPERIENCE
☎ 800-992-DIVE or 954/351-9889
Hours: daily
Admission charged
www.unexso.com

Visit UNEXSO for a close-up encounter with these marine mammals. UNEXSO (the Underwater Explorers Society) was established in 1965 and has led diving adventures and dolphin encounters around the world. The company offers several experiences, from a dolphin close encounter to a dolphin assistant trainer program, an all-day option that takes place offshore. Bring a swimsuit for these activities.

For people already signed up for other UNEXSO programs, the company offers special dive trips to see dolphins in their natural habitat and visit reefs (two tanks).

◆ TIP

Be sure to call for a reservation; slots for the special trips are extremely limited.

Horseback Riding

PINETREE STABLES
☎ 242/373-3600
E-mail: pinetree@batelnet.bs
www.bahamasvg.com

All levels of riders can enjoy these guided rides that take a 1½-hour look at the island, from beach to forest.

Windsurfing

You'll find windsurfing at both the **Luxaya Beach** and **Xanadu Beach**, with rentals costing anywhere from $15 to $25 per hour. Check with these operators:

CLARION ATLANTIK BEACH HOTEL
Lucaya Beach
☎ 242/373-1444

THE SWASHBUCKLER
Lucaya Beach
☎ 242/373-2909

PARADISE WATERSPORTS
Xanadu Beach
☎ 242/352-2887

Sailing

Grand Bahama has excellent marina facilities (many visitors arrive by boat, in fact). At the marinas, you'll find several operators who offers sailing (either crewed or small Sunfish you can man yourself), snorkel trips and glassbottom boat cruises. Check with these operators:

PARADISE WATERSPORTS
Freeport
☎ 242/352-2887

PAT AND DIANE TOURS
Freeport
☎ 242/373-8681

SUPERIOR WATERSPORTS
Freeport
☎ 242/373-4644

Snorkeling

BLUE HOLE SNORKELING SAFARIS
East End Adventures
☎ 242/373-6662
www.bahamasnet.com/eastendadventures
E-mail: safari@grouper.batelnet.bs

Grab your snorkel mask and see some of the most pristine sites in the region. The full-day tours offered by Blue Hole Snorkeling Safaris include a native-style lunch on an uninhabited island.

PARADISE WATERSPORTS
Freeport
☎ 242/352-2887
www.bahamasvg.com/paradise.html

Bring along your underwater camera for these trips!

This operator offers a "reef and wreck" snorkel trip. This is the only snorkel cruise of its type on the island. It takes passengers to Winky's Wreck, which sits in 40 feet of water. Prices cover gear (including a lifevest), instruction and refreshments. Allow about 1½ hours for the trip.

For nonswimmers, Paradise Watersports has got a glassbottom boat cruise so you can peek at the creatures of the deep.

PAT AND DIANE TOURS
Freeport
☎ 242/373-8681

Along with sunset sailing cruises, this operator offers snorkel tours lasting 1¾ hours. Tours take you to offshore reefs.

Scuba Diving

Scuba diving in Grand Bahama is synonymous with the Underwater Explorers Society (UNEXSO). The Society offers all types of dives: shark dives, reef dives and wreck dives. Most famous is **Theo's** **Wreck**, a steel freighter sunk by UNEXSO. For more information, contact UNEXSO (☎ 242/373-1244, fax 242/373-8956).

UNEXSO SHARK FEEDER PROGRAM
☎ 800/992-DIVE
Open daily
Admission: Free

Want to get up close and personal with sharks? Here is your chance. Only UNEXSO offers this unique four-day program, which is for scuba divers only. Participants wear a chainmail suit and dive in Shark Junction where they can hand-feed Caribbean reef sharks. You'll learn about shark petting and handling as well as the behaviour of these often-feared creatures. Price includes a personalized video, photo album, engraved wall plaque and mounted photo and equipment for all five dives.

Fishing

Fishing is big business on this island – everything from bonefishing on flies to deep-sea fishing for big guys like barracuda and kingfish. Check with these operators:

PARADISE WATERSPORTS
Freeport
☎ 242/352-2887

RUNNING MON MARINA AND RESORT
Freeport
☎ 242/352-6834

Golf

Grand Bahama Island is a golfer's destination – so much so it's known as the Golf Capital of the Bahamas.

REEF COURSE
The Lucayan, Lucaya
☎ 242/373-1066

This new course is designed by the Robert Trent Jones II group. The course, which is par 72, is considered challenging to experienced golfers because of water off the back tees. The front tees avoid water hazards and still have a spectacular view. For those readers who visited Grand Bahama in earlier years, this course is located at the site of the old Bahama Reef Golf Course.

THE LUCAYAN GOLF AND COUNTRY CLUB COURSE
The Lucayan, Lucaya
☎ 242/373/1066

Designed by Dick Wilson in 1962, this course is still considered one of the region's best. It was named among the top three in the Caribbean and the best in the Bahamas by *Golfweek* in 1998. Rated by USGA.

EMERALD AND RUBY COURSES
Resort at Bahamia
☎ 242/352-9661

Both par 72, these courses were designed by Dick Wilson and Joe Lee. Both are rated by USGA.

Tours

KAYAK NATURE TOURS
☎ 242/373-2485
http://bahamasvg.com/kayak.html
E-mail: kayaknat@grouper.batelnet.bs

Strolling the five-mile heritage path takes travelers back to the early days of Grand Bahama, before tourism, when this walk was one of the main thoroughfares on the island. Today it's quiet and lined with native plant species, butterflies and numerous birds. You'll also see the island's oldest building, The Hermitage.

Alternatively, grab a paddle and head off to see the natural side of Grand Bahama Island aboard a kayak. These all-day excursions travel Gold Rock Creek in the Lucayan National Park. Along with kayaking, you can snorkel and picnic on the trip and visit Lucayan caves.

Pedalers start at The Hermitage and bike along a wide trail on the way to Lucayan National Park, while birders will have the opportunity to spot 18 Bahamian species on these tours. You might see the red-legged thrush, the thick-billed vireo or even a fast-moving Cuban emerald hummingbird.

Shop Till You Drop

The Best Shops

JOHN BULL
International Bazaar, Freeport
☎ 242/352-2626

Most visitors find themselves in this shop in search of a Rolex watch because John Bull is an official Rolex retailer. If Rolex is not your sytle, choose from other upscale items such as gemstones, sunglasses and cosmetics.

Fine Jewelry

COLOMBIAN EMERALDS
International Bazaar, Freeport, ☎ 242/352-5380
Port Lucaya, Freeport, ☎ 242/373-2974
Resort at Bahamia, Freeport, ☎ 242/352-8291

This popular Caribbean boutique, with locations in Antigua, Aruba, Barbados, the Cayman Islands, Grenada, St. Lucia, St. Martin, the USVI and elsewhere, sells not only emeralds but other fine gemstones. All purchases include certified appraisals, 90-day insurance and full international guarantees.

Watches

CARTIER
International Bazaar, Freeport
☎ 242/352-5917

This boutique sells Cartier items exclusively. Choose from watches, belts and jewelry.

GUCCI
International Bazaar, Freeport
☎ 242/352-5380

Genuine Gucci goods such as perfume, shoes and leather products are for sale at this elegant boutique.

Perfumes & Cosmetics

THE PERFUME BAR
International Bazaar, Freeport
☎ 242/352-2165

Sells top-of-the-line skin care products, cosmetics and perfumes.

The Perfume Bar also has nine locations in & around Nassau.

Grog & Spirits

BUTLER & SANDS
Queen's Highway, Freeport
☎ 242/352-6627

An exclusive dealer of Bacardi rum, Butler & Sands carries imported wine, beer and liquors as well as locally made spirits.

Grand Bahama

Fashion Boutiques

FAR EAST TRADERS
International Bazaar, Freeport
☎ 242/352-9280

If you're looking for imports from the Orient, this is the place. Kimonos, tablecloths, silks and more can all be found at this unique store.

After Dark

Casino

RESORT AT BAHAMIA
Freeport
☎ 242/352-7811

There's a 20,000-square-foot casino at the Resort at Bahamia (formerly the Bahamas Princess), filled with everything from slots to stud poker. Tables feature craps, blackjack, roulette and more. There's also a sports book facility. Slots open at 9 a.m.; tables are available from 10 a.m. to 3 a.m.

Shows & Revues

CASINO ROYALE THEATRE
Resort at Bahamia
Freeport
☎ 242/352-7811

This Las Vegas-type revue has a dazzling show of song and dance; two shows are offered nightly except Mondays. The cover price includes a drink.

Dance Clubs

STUDIO 69
Midshipman Road, Lucaya
☎ 242/373-4824

This disco is open Thursday through Saturday nights; the cover price includes a drink. The crowd varies from night to night, but is almost always young.

West Indies Shows

CLUB WRLX
Queen's Highway
☎ 242/351-7663

This native show includes everything from fire dancing to limbo. Your entry fee includes a drink. The show is offered Thursday through Saturday nights. A good choice for first-time visitors to the Bahamas or the Caribbean.

Call for reservations at Club WRLX.

JOKERS WILD
Lucaya
☎ 242/373-7765

This nightclub offers a native show Sunday, Monday and Wednesday nights, with live music and dancing on the other nights. Tickets are available for the show only or for the show and dinner together. Again, this is a good show to attend if you've never seen one before.

Make reservations for a night at Jokers Wild.

Grand Bahama A-Z

Banks

Scotiabank
Regent Centre, Freeport
☎ 242/352-6774

Bank Of The Bahamas
Bank Lane and Woodstock Street, Freeport
☎ 242/352-7483

Dentists

Freeport Dental Centre
Pioneer's Professional Plaza, Freeport
☎ 242/352-4552

Grocery Store

Winn-Dixie
Downtown Shopping Centre, Freeport
☎ 242/352-7901

Emergency Phone Numbers

Emergencies	☎ 911
Hospital (Nassau)	☎ 322-2861 or 322-8411
Ambulance	☎ 322-2221
Med Evac	☎ 322-2881
Air Ambulance	☎ 327-7077
Fire	☎ 911
Police	☎ 911

Hospital

Sunrise Medical Centre
East Sunrise Highway
☎ 242/373-3333

Pharmacies

The Prescription Parlour Pharmacy
Eight Mile Rock
☎ 242/348-1155

Website

www.grand-bahama.com

Inagua

Inagua is actually two islands: Great and Little Inagua. They make up the fourth-largest island in the Bahamas and the southernmost point in the country. At 20 miles wide and 40 miles long, the island (referred to in the singular, despite being two islands) is scarcely populated, with just under 1,000 residents. But it has over 50,000 flamingos (more on that later).

Inagua is a favorite with birders, who come here to admire the flamingos & other birds.

★ DID YOU KNOW?

Inagua is an anagram of the word "iguana."

Inagua has a desert-like climate, with little rain, constant trade winds and little fresh water. This harsh environment is perfect for salt ponds, though, and those assets have brought money to local residents for many years. Salt was believed to have first motivated settlers to come to this island. In the 1930s Morton Salt Company dominated the salt industry around the globe and the company maintains a large operation here.

Great Inagua

NOT TO SCALE   © 2000 HUNTER PUBLISHING, INC

Today most residents work in the factory in **Matthew Town**, harvesting a million pounds of salt a year from the surrounding land.

Sunup to Sundown

Island Sightseeing

BAHAMAS NATIONAL PARK
East of Matthew Town in center of island

Sometimes called **Inagua National Park**, this 280-square-mile park is home to over 50,000 West Indian flamingos, the national bird of the Bahamas. The sanctuary is on 12-mile-long Lake Windsor, a brackish lake that's also home to Bahama parrots, cormorants, herons and egrets. One-day tours of the park are available; call the Bahamas National Trust in Nassau (☎ 242/393-1317) to obtain permission.

HENRI CHRISTOPHE PALACE
Northeast Point

Legend has it that a Haitian tyrant named Henri Christophe used Inagua as an escape destination when he fled Haiti. He built a summer palace on the island that still stands today. Word has it that the tyrant hit a cache of gold near the palace, a treasure never subsequently found.

Long Island

It's not hard to guess how this island got its name. Stretching 60 miles end to end (although only four

Long Island is visited by boaters, divers, anglers, and those in search of some quiet.

miles across) Long Island lives up to its moniker. This quiet getaway is a favorite with divers, anglers, and boaters and for those seeking quiet beaches, and a gentle, rolling landscape.

Like other Bahamian islands, this one was settled by many Loyalists who came here after the American Revolution. If you take a guided ride around the island, you'll see the ruins of several plantation homes that once were surrounded by large cotton estates.

While on your tour, you might stop by several other Long Island attractions. **Dunmore's Cave** was once used by pirates. You can also see the **Moorish-style churches** built by Father Jerome. Don't miss **Cape Santa Maria** on the north end of the island where Columbus first anchored and named this land Fernandina.

Best Places to Stay

CAPE SANTA MARIA BEACH RESORT AND FISHING CLUB
Stella Maris
☎ 242/338-5273, fax 242/338-6013
Reservations: ☎ 800/663-7090
E-mail: capesantamaria@batelnet.bs
www.obmg.com
Expensive to Deluxe

The 12 luxury accommodations here include one- and two-bedroom villas on a four-mile beach. The beachfront cottages have air conditioning. There are plenty of activities, including windsurfing, fishing, snorkeling and bicycling. Most guests spend their time either in or on the water. Both reef fishing and deep-sea fishing are very popular, and you might just land a marlin or barracuda!

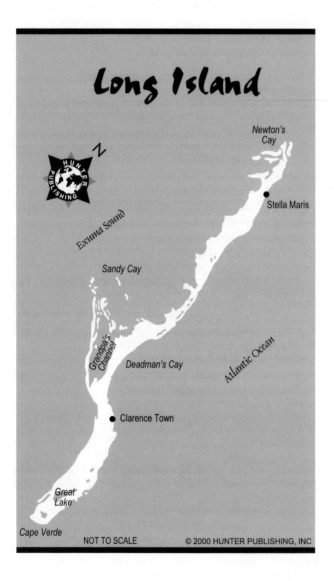

Long Island

STELLA MARIS INN
Stella Maris
☎ 242/338-2050, fax 242/338-2052
Reservations: ☎ 800-426-0466
E-mail: smrc@stellamarisresort.com
www.stellamarisresort.com
Moderate to Expensive

This 49-room resort has one-bedroom cottages and two- and four-bedroom villas. Rooms have a light island decor and are just steps from the sea. Some accommodations feature private pools. Each is air-conditioned and has ceiling fans and a refrigerator. Guests can enjoy snorkeling, scuba diving, fishing, cruises and sailing for a fee. There are plenty of free activities as well – daily land excursions, twice-weekly boat cruises, Sunfish sailing, biking and trips to beaches on the island's west coast.

Best Places to Eat

CAPE SANTA MARIA
Stella Maris
☎ 242/338-5273
Moderate to Expensive
Dress code: casually elegant
Reservations: required

Dine on Bahamian specialties as well as American and continental fare at this seaside restaurant. Meals are accompanied by a fine selection of wines. Breakfast, lunch and dinner are served but each at a preset time; call for times.

STELLA MARIS RESORT
CLUB DINING ROOM
Stella Maris Resort and Club
Stella Maris
☎ 242/338-2051
Moderate
Dress code: casually elegant
Reservations: suggested

In this garden setting, diners enjoy Bahamian, American and European food. The restaurant hosts many special events, such as barbecues and dinner cruises. The atmosphere is casual and fun. After dinner the resort usually offers dancing and music.

Sunup to Sundown

Scuba Diving

Long Island has several excellent dive sites; one of the best known is **Stella Maris Shark Reef**, a half-hour boat ride offshore. Divers descend to 20 or 30 feet, settle down on the sandy bottom, and hand-feed sharks. There are often over a dozen of the toothy critters ready and waiting!

STELLA MARIS RESORT
DIVE SHOP
Stella Maris
☎ 242/338-2055

Long Island

Fishing

BONAFIDE BONEFISHING
Stella Maris
☎ 242/338-2018

CAPE SANTA MARIA
Cape Santa Maria
☎ 242/338-5253

STELLA MARIS RESORT BONEFISHING
Stella Maris
☎ 242/338-2051

Long Island A-Z

Banks

Bank of Nova Scotia
Stella Maris
☎ 242/338-2000

Royal Bank of Canada
Grays
☎ 242/337-1044

Grocery Stores

J&M Food Store
Deadman's Cay
☎ 242/337-1446

Stella Maris General Store
Stella Maris
☎ 242/338-2020

Harding Supply Center
Salt Pond
☎ 242/338-0333

Emergency Phone Numbers

Emergencies . . . . ☎ 911
Hospital (Nassau) . ☎ 322-2861 or 322-8411
Ambulance . . . . ☎ 322-2221
Med Evac . . . . ☎ 322-2881
Air Ambulance . . . . ☎ 327-7077
Fire . . . . ☎ 911
Police . . . . ☎ 911

San Salvador

Most regard San Salvador as the site where Christopher Columbus first made landfall in the New World. (OK, the folks on Grand Turk in the Turks and Caicos will beg to differ, but more on that later.) When he landed he found an island named "Guanahani" by the Lucayan Indians. The explorer renamed the tiny isle San Salvador or Holy Savior.

⭐ **DID YOU KNOW?**

Exactly *where* Columbus landed is also up for debate, although most agree it was Long Bay, at a site now marked with a large stone cross.

San Salvador

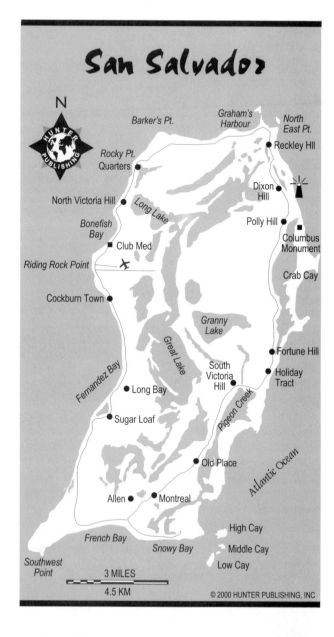

San Salvador

N

Barker's Pt.

Graham's Harbour

North East Pt.

Reckley Hll

Rocky Pt. Quarters

Dixon Hill

North Victoria Hill

Long Lake

Polly Hill

Bonefish Bay

Columbus Monument

Club Med

Riding Rock Point

Crab Cay

Cockburn Town

Granny Lake

Great Lake

Fortune Hill

South Victoria Hill

Holiday Tract

Fernandez Bay

Long Bay

Sugar Loaf

Pigeon Creek

Old Place

Atlantic Ocean

Allen

Montreal

High Cay

French Bay

Snowy Bay

Middle Cay

Southwest Point

Low Cay

3 MILES

4.5 KM

© 2000 HUNTER PUBLISHING, INC

The island became a lot less holy when notorious pirate Captain John Watling decided to set up camp here and proclaim the island his headquarters. The English buccaneer used San Salvador as a hideaway during the 17th century, but Watling's influence long outlived him, and the island took on the name Watling's Island. Finally, in 1925, the name of San Salvador was restored.

San Salvador attracts many scuba divers.

San Salvador is 200 miles east-southeast of Nassau and southeast of Cat Island. It is a favorite with scuba divers, offering visibility of up to 150 feet. The pace here remains quiet and relaxed. Most activity takes place in **Cockburn** (pronounced Ko-Burn) **Town**, a small community on the west coast.

Best Place to Stay

CLUB MED-COLUMBUS ISLE
Cockburn Town
☎ 242/331-2000, fax 242/331-2222
Reservations: ☎ 800/CLUB MED
www.clubmed.com
Moderate to Expensive (All-Inclusive)

Columbus Isle is a good choice for active travelers.

This all-inclusive resort is a favorite with people of all ages, although there are no facilities specifically for children. The 90-acre resort sprawls along a white sand beach and offers aerobics, bocce ball, deep-sea fishing, horseback riding, kayaking, sailing, snorkeling, scuba diving, softball, soccer, tennis, waterskiing, windsurfing. Columbus Isle also has a spa with massage and beauty treatments.

The resort is a colorful contrast to the surrounding turquoise waters, with yellow, pink and green cottages trimmed in gingerbread, each with a private balcony or patio.

San Salvador

Sunup to Sundown

PEOPLE-TO-PEOPLE PROGRAM
☎ 242/326-5371, ☎ 242/328-7810,
☎ 242/356-0435-8, fax 242/356-0434

To learn more about this unique cultural program, see page 89.

Island Sightseeing

DIXON HILL LIGHTHOUSE
Rum Cay
Hours: Daily (knock on the door)
Admission: Donation

The 1887 lighthouse is hand-operated, one of the last of its kind. You can climb the steep, winding stairs to the summit for a wonderful view of the surrounding waters, up to 19 miles on a clear day.

FARQUHARSON PLANTATION
OR BLACKBEARD'S CASTLE

This site features the most famous plantation ruins in the Bahamas. They're locally called Blackbeard's Castle, because it is rumored that the legendary pirate once stayed here. The ruins are worth a quick look, but will not take much of your time.

NEW WORLD MUSEUM
Blackwood Rock Point Beach, Palmetto Grove
Admission charged
Hours: Irregular (ask one of the locals if they can open the museum when you arrive)

New World Museum has some interesting Lucayan displays.

This museum has been in operation for 40 years and contains historic exhibits on the island. The collection is small and it won't take much time to see it all.

Scuba Diving

Excellent scuba diving sites are found around San Salvador, including reef and wreck dives at High Cay, Low Cay and Middle Cay. **The Great Cut**, a 40-130-foot dive, is a well known wall dive that features a cavern. Check with Club Med for dive packages.

San Salvador A-Z

Emergency Phone Numbers

Emergencies . . . . ☎ 911
Hospital (Nassau) . ☎ 322-2861 or 322-8411
Ambulance . . . . ☎ 322-2221
Med Evac . . . . ☎ 322-2881
Air Ambulance . . . . ☎ 327-7077
Fire . . . . ☎ 911
Police . . . . ☎ 911

Grocery Store

Last Chance Convenience Store
King Street, Rum Cay
☎ 242/331-2806

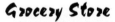

San Salvador

Turks & Caicos

Introduction

Mention to someone that you're headed to the Turks and Caicos and the first question you just might get is, "Where?" Few travelers seem to know of this secret treasure. Some think it has a connection with the country of Turkey. But this chain of islands is an increasingly popular vacation destination for anglers, scuba divers, and those in search of a little peace and quiet.

Tourism & Development

Word is getting out, though, and fast. The future of tourism in the Turks and Caicos Islands is easily summed up by the Honorable Oswald Skippings, Minister of Tourism, who says, "We are on a roll."

Statistics back up that claim. Visitor arrivals have soared to 100,000 annually. Construction projects dot the islands, especially Providenciales.

Predictions call for even more promotion of tourism thanks to a new partnership between the islands and American Express through the American Express Official Card Program. One of 24 partners in the program, the Turks and Caicos expects to receive worldwide attention.

"While many think of the Turks and Caicos as one of the Caribbean's best-kept secrets, we intend to change that and to get the word out," explained Mary Kay Gaines, Head of Destination Business for American Express Cards.

Plans call for focusing not just on Providenciales, but on the Turks and Caicos as a whole. "We have eight wonderful inhabited islands and we tend to forget that Providenciales is not the only one. This year we hope to place emphasis on the ones not getting the attention of Provo," said Caesar Campbell, Director of Tourism.

Development will take place on many of the outlying areas. East Caicos will be the recipient of one of the largest projects, a $350 million development that will include a cruise port large enough to accommodate up to eight cruise ships. The currently uninhabited island is to offer a five-star hotel, watersports center and golf course.

Long-term plans for East Caicos include construction of seven additional resorts on the island's north shore. "We are not looking to develop mass tourism," said Skippings. "The government's aim is to create sustainable tourism and promote growth that is sensitive to and in harmony with the environment."

Location

The Turks and Caicos (pronounced Cay-Cos) are just 1½ hours by plane from Miami, tucked halfway between the tip of Florida and Puerto Rico. This British crown colony, ruled by a governor appointed by the Queen, is better known to the world of banking than among travelers. With its tax-free status, use of the English language and the US dollar as official currency, and with the stability of the British government backing the islands, the Turks and Caicos have been a popular off-shore banking center with American corporations for many years.

We found that the same attributes that make these islands so attractive to businesses also make them appealing to travelers. A trip to the islands is quick, thanks to daily jet service from Miami. Once there, travel around the islands, although on the left side of the road, is easy, and you don't need to use foreign currency or calculate exchange rates. And the political stability of this government has brought a sense of security to the Turks and Caicos, resulting in an incredibly low rate of crime.

Beaches are safe and uncrowded, and tourists can enjoy late-night walks from property to property on the beaches of the main island, Providenciales.

History

History buffs will find reason enough to take a day trip to Grand Turk to visit the **Turks and Caicos National Museum** (☎ 649-946-2160), home of the oldest authenticated European shipwreck in the New World. The main exhibit features the Molasses Reef shipwreck, which occurred in the Turks and Caicos nearly 500 years ago. The Spanish caravel hit the reef and quickly sank in only 20 feet of water, where it remained until the 1970s. The museum, located in a 150-year-old house on the island's main street, features artifacts from the wreck with interactive displays, video presentations and scientific exhibits.

The Islands

Although the chain is composed of nearly 40 limestone islands, only eight are considered destinations. **Providenciales**, or Provo, is home to about 6,000 residents and to most of the tourist industry. The capital of the Turks and Caicos is the island of **Grand Turk**, a short hop from Provo. This seven-mile-square island has some historic buildings and the national museum, a must-see for history buffs.

Other inhabited islands include **North Caicos**, the most verdant island in the chain; **South Caicos**, a fishing center; **Middle Caicos**, home of several sea caves; and **Salt Cay**, a tiny island of only 300 residents that was once the world's largest producer of sea salt.

The Attractions

For now, the Turks and Caicos are uncrowded with either residents or tourists. Just how uncrowded these islands are is very obvious when arriving in Providenciales, better known as simply Provo. Although this island boasts the largest portion of the Turks and Caicos population of 15,000, it is still open and unsettled – one of its biggest attractions for those looking to see the islands "the way they used to be." This sickle-shaped island sports scrubby growth, short palms and climbing sea grapes. Limestone roads wind across the flat island.

Highrises are forbidden on Provo. Resorts may be built no taller than three stories.

But the traveler to Provo will soon realize that beaches and clear waters that are the main attractions.

You won't find beach vendors or hagglers on these shores, just a few tourists and locals enjoying snorkeling or a swim in the gentle surf.

For most visitors, the real attraction of the Turks and Caicos is the luxury of being able to do nothing at all.

Scuba Diving & Snorkeling

Days are spent on the beach or in water so clear that it is often cited as one of the top scuba destinations in the world, thanks to a reef system 65 miles across and 200 miles long. Visibility averages 80 to 100 feet or better, and the water temperature ranges from 82 to 84° in the summer and 75-76° in the winter months. Beneath the calm waves swim colorful marine animals as exotic as hawksbill turtles, nurse sharks and octopi. With a one-mile vertical coral wall offshore, Provo is a diver's paradise.

Grand Turk offers miles of drop-off diving, while South Caicos provides many ledge and wall dives. Wreck divers can explore the *HMS Endymion,* a ship that went down in a storm in 1790, leaving behind cannons and anchors for divers to view off Salt Cay. One of the more unusual dive sites that is visible from the air is the Blue Hole, a depression hundreds of feet deep in the reef off Middle Caicos. It is filled with pelagics, including sharks, rays and groupers.

⭐ **DID YOU KNOW?**

Touching coral causes the organism to die. Swim with care!

Ecotourism

From December through April, ecotourists journey to Salt Cay for a chance to spot humpback whales, watching for the giant mammals from shore or in the water in scuba gear. Ecotravelers can enjoy bird watching on North Caicos or watching gentle rock iguanas on Little Water Cay, home of a new nature trail program, one of 33 nature reserves and refuges in the Turks and Caicos. Raised boardwalks and observation towers allow visitors to see the iguanas in their natural habitat. Trips to Little Water Cay are offered by several operators who also schedule full-day excursions to the inhabited but sparsely developed islands of North and Middle Caicos for viewing a pink flamingo colony, talking with local residents, and enjoying a beach barbecue. Monthly "glow worm" cruises are another unique experience for travelers. Scheduled from three to six nights after a full moon, these cruises take visitors to the Caicos Bank for a look at a phosphorescent marine worm that lights the waters about an hour after sunset in a unusual mating ritual.

To protect the ecology of the islands, the Turks and Caicos have established an extensive national park and nature reserve system. Over 31 national parks dot the islands, including Provo's **Princess Alexandra National Park**, which has 13 miles of protected beaches. The **NW Point Marine**, another park, offers spectacular wall diving, and **Chalk Sound** has small boat sailing on the west end of the island.

Vacationers are certain to spot wildlife on daytrips to nearby Water Cay. Located northeast of Provo, this small island is the home of numerous iguanas that greet boat passengers and happily pose for photos just yards away. Snorkeling cruises take visitors from Provo to this island most every afternoon.

◆ *NOTE*

National park rules make it illegal to hunt and fish; remove any animal or coral; moor vessels over 60 feet except on fixed buoys; or drive boats within 100 yards of the shoreline.

JoJo the Dolphin

The best-known natural attraction of these islands is JoJo, a wild dolphin and the mascot of the Turks and Caicos. This Atlantic bottlenose dolphin has been sighted for 12 years along the north coast of Provo, the only case ever documented of prolonged interaction between an individual wild dolphin and humans. Often spotted swimming along the north shore or near boats, JoJo is protected and the government has declared him a national treasure.

JoJo has his own website: www.jojo.pc. The JoJo Project pays for medical costs associated with the dolphin and memberships are available for $50 from the JoJo Project, PO Box 153, Providenciales, Turks and Caicos or by calling or faxing ☎ 649/941-5617.

Another unique attraction is the Caicos Conch Farm on Provo, the only farm in the world that raises queen conch, the shellfish that's become a favorite meal throughout much of the Caribbean. A guided tour offers a look at the conch in various stages, from the larvae in the hatchery to adulthood.

The Cost

The Alive Price Scale

$ Prices change as quickly as the sand shifts on a beach. In addition, accommodations offer a wide variety of steps in their price scale. Partial ocean view, full ocean view, oceanside, garden view – each has its own price based on the month and the day of the week.

For accommodations, our price scale is designed to give you a ballpark figure for a typical stay during peak season. We've based these estimates on high season for a standard room for two persons. Prices are given in US dollars (but, hey, currency conversion is as simple as it gets – one US dollar is always equal to one Bahamian dollar).

> ◆ **NOTE**
>
> These figures don't take into account additional amenities such as meal plans, dive packages, etc.

Price Scale - Accommodations

Based on a standard room for two in high season. Prices are given in US dollars.

Deluxe . . . . Over $300
Expensive . . . . $201-$300
Moderate . . . . $100-$200
Inexpensive . . . . Under $100

All our hotel selections take major credit cards, are air conditioned and have private baths, except in the case of the few guest houses where noted.

At any hotel, be sure to conserve water, a precious commodity.

For an all-inclusive, where meals, drinks, tips, transportation and sometimes even more is included, prices are given per person for adults based on double occupancy.

For dining, our price scale is based on a three-course dinner, including appetizer or soup, entrée, dessert and coffee. Cocktails and wine are extra. Price estimates are per person in US funds.

Price Scale - Dining

Per person, excluding drinks, service and tip. Prices are in US dollars.

Expensive . . . . Over $30
Moderate . . . . $10-$30
Inexpensive . . . . Under $10

Restaurants at All-Inclusive Resorts

All-inclusive resorts often open their doors to non-guests. We've included the local telephone number of the resort so just give them a call and ask about purchasing a day pass.

Getting There

The Turks and Caicos Islands have three international airports: **Providenciales, Grand Turk** and **South Caicos**. Most visitors arrive in Providenciales. Small domestic airports are found on the other islands, except for East and West Caicos, both uninhabited.

Twice-daily jet service to Providenciales is available on **American Airlines** (☎ 800-433-7300) from Miami. Flying time is approximately 80 minutes. Inter-island scheduled service is available on **Turks and Caicos Airways** (☎ 649-946-4255).

Inter-island charters and charters to other Caribbean islands can be booked on **Interisland Airways** (☎ 649-941-5481) or **SkyKing** (☎ 649-941-KING).

Planning Your Trip

Types of Accommodations

The Turks and Caicos Islands currently offers a total of 1,500 guest rooms, most found on Providenciales. Accommodations range from full-service resorts to small properties and guesthouses.

Where Should We Go?

The Turks and Caicos are more than one vacation destination. So where should you go? You will probably be arriving in Providenciales at the international airport. This island is the home base for most travelers and attracts scuba divers, snorkelers, nature lovers and anyone looking to get away from it all. It has accommodations to suit couples, families and singles. If you're looking for quiet seclusion, excellent eco-tourism adventures, and are willing to vacation with fewer entertainment options, the other islands make good choices.

Choosing a Resort Area

Here's a rundown of the various destinations in the Turks and Caicos:

PROVIDENCIALES
Population: 6,000
Size: 38 square miles

The top tourist destination in the Turks and Caicos, Provo is home to the largest selection of resorts, restaurants and activities. An excellent destination for scuba divers, anglers and those looking for tranquility with all the amenities of a larger destination.

GRAND TURK
Population: 4,300
Size: 6 square miles

The capital of the Turks and Caicos is a destination favored by scuba divers and anglers.

NORTH CAICOS
Population: 1,300
Size: 41 square miles

The most lush island in this chain makes a good day trip from Provo and is also a popular destination for those in search of peace and quiet.

SOUTH CAICOS
Population: 1,200
Size: 8 square miles

South Caicos is considered to be the capital of the Turks and Caicos fishing industry. The quiet island getaway has few distractions.

MIDDLE CAICOS
Population: 300
Size: 48 square miles

This quiet, cave-pocked island can be seen on a day trip and also offers an accommodation. A good destination for sportfishermen and divers.

SALT CAY
Population: 300
Size: 2½ square miles

The smallest of the Turks and Caicos islands, this was once the capital of the area's sea salt industry. Today it offers a very lavish hotel and smaller accommodations that are often tailored to meet the needs of divers.

EAST CAICOS
Population: uninhabited
Size: 18 square miles

East Caicos is a good day trip from Grand Turk or Provo. It offers secluded beaches, scuba diving and sportfishing.

PINE CAY
Population: private
Size: 800 acres

This private island is home to an environmentally sensitive resort.

Getting Ready

Travelers' Information, A-Z

Banking

The Turks and Caicos is fast emerging in the international banking world, much like the Cayman Islands, so you'll have no shortage of banking facilities on Provo.

Barclays and Bank of Nova Scotia are both on Provo. Bank hours are 8:30-12:30 and 2-4:30, Monday through Thursday, and 8-12:30 and 2-4:30 on Friday.

On the smaller islands banking options are limited.

Climate

Summer highs average about 90°; winter highs about 75°. The hottest months are August to November, when the trade winds drop and days can be sultry.

Currency

The US dollar is the official currency of Turks and Caicos.

Customs

Vacationers may bring in one carton of cigars or cigarettes, one bottle of liquor or wine and perfume for personal use.

Credit Cards

Major credit cards are accepted at most establishments.

Departure Tax

There is a departure tax of $15 per person, excluding children under 12 years.

Driving

Driving is British style, on the left side of the road. A valid driver's license from the US or an international license may be used to drive. There is a vehicle rental tax of $10 for cars and $5 for scooters.

Electricity

Throughout these islands the standard is 120/240 volts/60 cycles.

Entry Requirements

US visitors are required to have proof of citizenship such as an official birth certificate or voter registration card and photo identification, or a passport. Visitors must also show a return ticket. Visitors from other countries must possess a valid passport.

Hospital

Grand Turk is home to a 36-bed hospital. Provo has medical clinics as well as a hyperbaric chamber.

Language

English is the official language of the Turks and Caicos Islands.

Pets

Incoming pets must have all required shots and a veterinarian's certificate.

Telephone

Good phone service is available from these islands, but it is very expensive. You will find that it is cheaper to have parties call you from home or to send a fax. A phone card is needed to use telephone booths. These come in $5, $10 and $20 denominations and can be purchased at the Cable and Wireless offices, as well as at island stores.

Time Zone

The Turks and Caicos are on Eastern Standard Time. From April through October, daylight saving time is observed.

Tipping

A tip of 15% is standard for restaurant service.

Tourism Office

For information on the islands, ☎ 800/241-0824 or write **Turks and Caicos Tourist Office,** 11645 Biscayne Boulevard, Suite 302, North Miami, FL 33181. The local number is ☎ 305/891-4117, fax 305/891-7096.

On-island, the tourism office is **Turks and Caicos Islands Tourist Board,** PO Box 128, Grand Turk, Turks and Caicos Islands, ☎ 649/946-2321, fax 649/946-2733.

Vaccinations

No vaccinations or immunizations are required to visit the Turks and Caicos Islands.

Water

Water is safe to drink throughout the islands.

Website

The official Turks and Caicos website is www.turksandcaicostourism.com.

Warnings

With their small populations, these islands have a low crime rate. However, as in any destination, take common-sense precautions while traveling.

- ✆ Don't leave valuables on the beach while you swim;

- ✆ Use hotel safes for your valuables;

- ✆ Be aware of your surroundings, especially during the evening hours.

While You're There

Festivals

For dates and additional information on the festivals of the Turks and Caicos, contact the Tourist Board at ☎ 800/241-0824, 305/891-4117 or 679/946-2321.

☀ January

New Year's Day, public holiday. All islands.

☼ March

Commonwealth Day, public holiday. This event takes place on a Monday in early March; expect all public offices to be closed. All islands.

Spring Garden Festival, Grand Turk. Held during easter, this festival includes kite flying, a candlelight ceremony on Good Friday, a local restaurant competition and a fish fry. Held in late March.

☼ May

The Regatta is a great event for sailing buffs!

Regatta, South Caicos. This late-May event includes a beauty pageant, sailboat races (call the Tourist Board for entry details) and plenty of local food.

National Heroes Day, a public holiday, is celebrated in late May. Expect most offices to be closed this day.

☼ June

Queen's Official Birthday Celebrations, Grand Turk. On this public holiday in early June, government offices close. (The actual date varies, but it is always on a Monday.) The island celebrates with special events that include a uniformed parade (and we mean uniforms – everyone from the police force to the Girl Scouts and Boy Scouts takes to the streets) and medals from Her Majesty the Queen are given out by the governor.

Fun in the Sun, Salt Cay. Just what is fun in the sun? How about a beauty pageant for the youngest residents of Salt Cay, along with dances and local food. This celebration is a good way to meet the handful of people who call this island home. The festival, held in late June, has a real small town feel.

☀ July

Festarama, North Caicos. This mid-July celebration features local bands and sports.

Provo Summer Festival, Provo. Held in late July, this event includes the Miss Turks and Caicos beauty pageant as well as dingy races and parades.

Grand Turk Fishing Tournament, Grand Turk. This annual event begins with parties, a beach volleyball tournament and music, before getting down to the serious business of fishing. Competitors vie for a top prize of $5,000. To compete, anglers must register and pay entry fees before the start of the event in late July. For information, ☎ 649/946-2504.

☀ August

Middle Caicos Expo, Middle Caicos. The Expo features beauty pageants, boat races and sports in mid-August.

Rake and Scrape Music Festival, Grand Turk. Mid-August. As the name says, this event features plenty of "rake and scape" or music produced using drums and hand saws. Great for music lovers.

Cactusfest, Grand Turk. This festival features parades, local bands and games. It's held in late August. A good way to experience the fun and excitement of a small island festival.

☀ September

National Youth Day, all islands. Local youth are spotlighted at this sporting event held in late September.

☼ October

Turks and Caicos Amateur Open Golf Championship, Provo. This 36-hole, two-day championship is open to visitors. Contact the Tourism Board for details or the **Provo Golf Club** (☎ 649/946-5991, fax 649/946-5992). The championship takes place in mid-October.

Columbus Day, October 13. This is a public holiday; expect businesses to be closed. All islands.

International Human Rights Day, October 24. This is a public holiday; expect businesses to be closed. All islands.

☼ November

Remembrance Day, Grand Turk. November 2.

Guy Fawkes Day, all islands. November 5. Guy Fawkes attempted to bomb British Parliament in 1605 as a cry for religious freedom. King James was inside the building at the time. Fawkes' plan failed and he was executed.

☼ December

Christmas Tree Lighting Ceremony, Grand Turk. In early December this public lighting of the island Christmas tree kicks off the start of the holiday season.

Christmas Day, December 25. Public holiday.

Boxing Day, December 26. This public holiday is a reminder of the times when servants boxed leftover food and enjoyed their own celebration the day after the Christmas festivities.

Watch Night, December 31. All islands. This long-time tradition includes an all-night church service with the ringing of bells to welcome in the New Year.

Getting Around

By Rental Car

Rental cars are available, but they can be tough to obtain and expensive –about $45 a day for economy size, $59 for a full-size. Once you have a rental car, you'll find that gasoline prices are equally expensive: about $2.50 a gallon.

By Taxi

Taxi service is good on the islands, especially on Provo. There, you can call the **Paradise Taxi Company** (☎ 13555) or the **Provo Taxi Association** (☎ 65481). **Nell's Taxi and Tours** (☎ 13228 or 10051) offers island tours at $25 per hour and dinner transportation for $6 per person round-trip to any island restaurant (minimum four persons).

Shopping

Turks and Caicos may have a lot of attributes that appeal to vacationers, but, with few exceptions, shopping isn't one of them. You will find limited shopping on Provo, most in a complex called Ports of Call, designed to resemble an old Caribbean seaside town. Look for restaurants, crafts and art in this new development near Grace Bay.

Favorite Purchases

Conch (pronounced KonK) shells make a wonderful souvenir from these islands. Stop by the **Conch Farm** on Provo to purchase a beautiful shell; you'll also find some large piles next to several island bars where you can stop and make an inexpensive purchase.

For **Caribbean art**, check out the **Bamboo Gallery** on Provo, an excellent gallery that's been featured in many newspaper and magazine articles. Here you'll find Haitian, Jamaican and even some Turks and Caicos artwork. Near Ports of Call, **Maison Creole** also has magnificent artwork with crafts from Haiti and other Caribbean islands.

Providenciales

Providenciales is open and unsettled, dotted with short palms and sea grapes. Chalky limestone roads wind across the flat land, connecting settlements like Blue Hills and The Bight.

But the traveler to Provo will soon realize that its desert terrain is just a backdrop to the clear waters and long beaches that are the main attractions. These sandy stretches can be miles long, dotted only with the footprints of animals and birds. You won't find beach vendors or hagglers on these shores, just a few tourists and locals. Highrises are forbidden, with resorts built no taller than three stories.

But most visitors come to Provo to do nothing at all. Days are spent on the beach or in the clear waters of the ocean.

This is a popular dive destination, with good visibility and warm waters that are home to hawksbill turtles, nurse sharks, octopi.

With the high number of both American visitors and expatriates in the Turks and Caicos, you'll find many cuisines represented on the islands.

◆ TIP

For a taste of true island food, sample the conch, served as fritters, salads and sandwiches, as well as grouper, hogfish, soft-shell crab and spiny lobster.

Providenciales

Best Places to Stay

There are almost 1,500 accommodations in the Turks and Caicos, most found on Providenciales. They range from full-service resorts to small properties and guesthouses.

ALLEGRO RESORT AND CASINO TURKS AND CAICOS
☎ 649/949-5555, fax 649/949-5629
Reservations: ☎ 800/858-2258
www.allegroresorts.com
Moderate to Expensive (All-Inclusive)

The Allegro Resort is the former Turquoise Reef Resort, always a favorite accommodation on Provo and

The Allegro property recently underwent a $22.5 million renovation with its purchase by Allegro Resorts.

well known for its great beach and extensive watersports.

This 250-room resort is an all-inclusive, which incorporates all meals (including dinners at two specialty restaurants featuring Italian and Caribbean cuisine), alcoholic beverages, nightly entertainment, non-motorized watersports such as kayaking and sailing, scuba clinic, tennis, and a kids club for ages four to 12. For additional fees, you can arrange waterskiing, jet skiing, parasailing, scuba trips and golf.

The Allegro Resort has the only casino in the Turks and Caicos.

All rooms at this fun-loving resort have views of the sea or the gardens and also feature a balcony, air-conditioning and cable TV.

BEACHES TURKS AND CAICOS RESORT AND SPA
☎ 649/946-8000, fax 649/946-8001
Reservations: ☎ 800/BEACHES
www.beaches.com
Moderate to Expensive (All-Inclusive)

Part of the Sandals family of resorts, this is a favorite with families. Located on the 12-mile beach at Grace Bay, this 224-room resort is open to singles, couples and families.

It has a variety of restaurants. Reflections is the main dining room and features buffet servings of breakfast, lunch and dinner. Sapodilla's and Schooners serve adults only, while families are welcome in the Arizona Bar and Grill for Tex-Mex cuisine or the Teppanyaki restaurant Kimonos.

Children may be left in supervised areas where they are entertained. A nursery is available for infants and toddlers, while the Cuda Kids Club keeps older children happy with a children's pool, gazebo, playground, table tennis and pool table facilities. Kids' classes offer everything from sandcastle building to reggae singing. Video game buffs will love the Sega Center with state-of-the-art video games (all complimentary). Teens also have special activities, including disco nights, movie nights, sports tournaments and more.

This Sandals resort is great for families & those looking for a spa experience.

Beaches Turks and Caicos Resort and Spa offers 200 guest rooms and suites. It contributed greatly to the recognition of the Turks and Caicos as a destination for many travelers. Part of the Sandals family, this all-inclusive welcomes families, couples and singles. Guest facilities include a dive shop, fitness center, spa, tennis and children's program. Meeting facilities for up to 185 attendees are also available.

Providenciales

CLUB MED-TURKOISE
☎ 800/258-2633, 649/946-5500, fax 649/946-5501
www.clubmed.com
Moderate (All-Inclusive)

Along with Beaches, the Club Med is the most action-packed place in the Turks and Caicos. This all-inclusive has welcomed guests for over 15 years.

Guests at Club Med-Turkoise must be 18 years or over.

Located on Grace Bay Beach, the 298-room resort is popular with singles and couples. The hotel has a dive center (extra charge for scuba diving) as well as other watersports, tennis, fitness center, nightclub, and more. There's plenty of other fun: circus workshops, deep-sea fishing, sailing, soccer, softball, volleyball – you name it.

Club Med is very popular with singles.

The resort offers three restaurants and day and night passes can be purchased.

COMFORT SUITES TURKS AND CAICOS
Grace Bay
☎ 649/946-8888, fax 649/946-5444
Reservations: ☎ 800/992-2015
Inexpensive

This latest addition to the lodging scene is adjacent to Ports of Call shopping center. The 99-room property offers king and two double bed accommodations; rooms include a sofabed and small refrigerator as well. There is no restaurant on-site, although a complimentary continental breakfast is served daily and several restaurants are located at Ports of Call.

Comfort Suites is a good budget choice.

We stayed here recently and found the atmosphere pleasant and the property well located. It's nothing fancy, but it's good value. Rooms are pretty much like those you'd find in a Comfort Suite property in the US, and it's very convenient. We started every day with breakfast at one of the Ports of Call restaurants, strolled to the beaches at Grace Bay in the afternoon, and enjoyed nightlife either at the casino just across the street at Allegro at night or at one of the clubs at Ports of Call.

EREBUS INN
Turtle Cove
☎ 649/946-4240, fax 649/946-4704
Reservations: ☎ 800/645-1179
Moderate

Overlooking Turtle Cove Marina, this modest inn is a charming spot for those on a budget – plus, it offers a great view. Amenities include a gym and a freshwater pool as well as an excellent restaurant.

GRACE BAY CLUB

Grace Bay
☎ 869/946-5757, fax 649/946-5758
Reservations: ☎ 800/946-5050
www.gracebayclub.com
Expensive to Deluxe

Provo's most exclusive property is this Swiss-owned hotel with a high regard for privacy. Furnished with items from Mexico and India, the rooms are decorated in subdued beige tones to put the emphasis on the brilliant color of the sea just beyond the balcony.

Outside, the Grace Bay Club also exudes an elegant look. The Spanish-style buildings, with their terra-cotta tiled roofs and stone columns, contrast with the blue sea and the brilliant hibiscus and bougainvillea that provide tropical color.

Guests enjoy many watersports here, from quiet Sunfish sails to snorkeling in the pristine waters. Scuba diving, bonefishing, sea kayaking and sailing excursions can also be arranged.

Accommodations include 21 guest suites with private balconies on the oceanfront. All have cable television, air conditioning, in-room safes, fax machines upon request, ceiling fans, kitchen facilities with refrigerator and ice maker, washer and dryer, twice-daily maid service, room service, marbled baths and hair dryers. There are tennis courts and bicycles for guest use. The resort is also home to the gourmet Anacaona restaurant.

Providenciales

The Grace Bay Club is a very elegant property offering a quiet atmosphere & upscale accommodations.

LE DECK
Grace Bay
☎ 649/946-5547, fax 649/946-5770
Reservations: ☎ 800/528-1905
Moderate

Le Deck has comfortable rooms sporting a recent refurbishment, an excellent restaurant and a central location. It's nothing fancy, but you can't beat the Grace Bay location. The beachfront property has a freshwater swimming pool.

OCEAN CLUB
Grace Bay
☎ 649/946-5880, fax 649/946-5845
Reservations: ☎ 800/457-8787
www.ocean-club.com; www.oceanclubwest.com
Moderate to Expensive

Two children under age 12 can stay with parents free in the same suite at the Ocean Club.

Starting as a simple timeshare property, the Ocean Club has grown to full resort status with a small shopping arcade, convenience store, watersports concession, restaurant, beach grill and two bars.

The all-suite facility still functions as a timeshare, but is also available to regular guests. It sits alongside other full-service resorts on a 12-mile stretch of beach.

Expansive rooms greet even those guests who chose the smaller accommodations at Ocean Club. With white tile floors, wicker furnishings, sliding glass doors opening to screened patios and balconies and numerous windows, suites here are sunny and styled in casual beachfront decor.

Every room has air conditioning, fully equipped kitchens or kitchenettes, cable TV, direct dial phones with voice messaging, in-suite washer and dryer and daily maid service. Family-friendly features such as rollaway beds, baby cribs and high chairs are available.

The resort's white sand beach is one of its top assets, located just steps from the suites. Water lovers can also choose from two freshwater pools, including a freeform pool that's a favorite with young vacationers. Art Pickering's **Provo Turtle Divers**, located at the resort, offers dive excursions and watersports, including snorkel trips, bonefishing and deep-sea fishing, parasailing, scuba certification and more.

Ocean Club is a great choice for families & anyone who want kitchen facilities.

Guest facilities include a fitness center with stationary bikes, Universal equipment, Stair Climbers and free weights. Massages and aromatherapy are available at the fitness center or in-room with the Ocean Club's licensed therapist.

Tennis is available day and night on a lighted court.

The Ocean Club provides 83 units with full kitchens, screen balconies and porches. Guest amenities include tennis, a fitness room, watersports, dive shop, nearby golf and the Gecko Grill restaurant with a Culinary Institute of America-trained chef.

Gecko Grill is a great restaurant!

Providenciales

Ocean Club West

The property is in the process of adding Ocean Club West, located next to Grace Bay Club. Facing the white, sandy shores of Grace Bay Beach, the resort will have 90 condominium-style suites, an expansive Caribbean-style freeform pool with an island and swim-up bar, the Seaside Café (an oceanfront restaurant and bar), a fitness center, tennis courts, watersports center and dive shop.

The first phase consists of five of the seven accommodation buildings, the dive and watersports shop, the Seaside Café and a freshwater pool. The resort will have impeccable landscaping. Remaining phases, which will be complete by October of 2000, include the development of two additional accommodation buildings, tennis courts and lobby. For reservations or more about this new addition, visit www.oceanclubwest. com.

TURTLE COVE INN
Turtle Cove
☎ 649/946-4203, fax 649/946-4141
Reservations: ☎ 800/887-0477
Inexpensive to Moderate

When divers come up for air, many head to this resort, where they find an on-site dive center and packages including two-tank morning dives. Located directly off the marina, rooms here are simple but include telephone, cable TV and a private balcony. A freshwater pool is available for guests, along with a casual restaurant and bar.

Best Places to Eat

ANACAONA
Grace Bay Club
☎ 649/946-5050
Expensive
Dress code: dressy
Reservations: recommended

Save one night for a special dinner at Anacaona, an Indian word that translates into "feather of gold." This open-air restaurant is true gold, a gem of a property that combines European elegance with Caribbean tranquillity. Enjoy an elegant meal beneath a thatched palapa which rests on Roman columns. The menu is complemented with an extensive wine list and Cuban cigars.

ANGELA'S DELICATESSEN
Ports of Call
☎ 649/946-5023
Inexpensive
Dress code: casual
Reservations: not required

Dine inside in a pub-like atmosphere or outdoors under an umbrella at this deli. It serves sandwiches and light meals, including breakfast.

ARIZONA BAR AND GRILL
Beaches Resort and Spa
☎ 649/946-8000
All Inclusive
Dress code: casual
Reservations: not required

The Arizona Bar and Grill, decorated to look like it came right out of the desert Southwest, is one of the more popular dining options at Beaches.

Grilled dishes – chicken fajitas, barbecue ribs and Tex-Mex – are favorite options. During the day, Arizona offers burgers made to order.

BANANA BOAT CARIBBEAN GRILL
Turtle Cove
☎ 649/946-5706
Moderate
Dress code: casual
Reservations: not required

This waterside, open-air eatery serves local dishes right at the Turtle Cove Marina. Start off with Caribbean nachos (red, blue and yellow corn chips with three cheeses, jalapeños, guacamole, sour cream and jerk spice), conch fritters or potato skins, then move on to such entrées as Caicos lobster or the chicken in Paradise (grilled chicken with pineapple, mozzarella and a Caicos-spiced mayonnaise).

BAREFOOT CAFE
Ports of Call
☎ 349/946-5282
Inexpensive
Dress code: casual
Reservations: not required

Breakfast is served all day at the Barefoot Café.

On a recent trip to Provo, we stayed at the Comfort Inn and started every morning with breakfast at the nearby Barefoot Café. The specialty is the "eggle bagel," with bacon, cheese and egg.

Homemade pastries, egg salad croissants and The Western (scrambled eggs with tomato and onion on a baguette) are other specialties.

CAICOS CAFE
Governor's Road, Grace Bay
☎ 649/946-5278
Moderate to Expensive
Dress code: casual
Reservations: suggested

You can dine on fresh seafood grilled just steps away from your table at this outdoor eatery. We enjoyed a dinner here of jerk chicken (super hot!) and conch chowder.

Steak, lamb and barbecue dishes are also available, along with grouper, duck breast and escargots.

COCO BISTRO
Grace Bay Road
☎ 649/946-5369
Moderate to Expensive
Dress code: casually elegant
Reservations: suggested

This indoor and outdoor restaurant specializes in Mediterranean dishes served with Spanish wines. The outdoor tables are shaded by a coconut grove (a unique sight in Provo).

Coco Bistro is open for dinner only.

DORA'S RESTAURANT AND BAR
Leeward Highway
☎ 649/946-4558
Inexpensive to Moderate
Dress code: casual
Reservations: not required

Local dishes are the specialty at Dora's, which serves three meals daily. On Monday and Thursday nights enjoy a seafood buffet, while live music on Saturday nights brings in many late-night guests.

FAIRWAYS BAR AND GRILL
Provo Golf Course
☎ 649/946-5991
Moderate
Dress code: golfwear
Reservations: not required

Breakfast and lunch (as well as dinner Tuesday through Saturday) are served at this nice clubhouse overlooking the greens. The restaurant is part of a West Indies-style clubhouse and is generally filled with golfers enjoying sandwiches, salads, fish dishes and an extensive selection of Caribbean drinks.

Providenciales

GECKO GRILLE
Ocean Club
☎ 649/946-5880
Moderate to Expensive
Dress code: casually elegant
Reservations: suggested

Start with a drink at the bar then choose an indoor or outdoor table. We always dine outside beneath the ficus trees, lit with small, white Christmas lights.

Very impressive at the Gecko Grille is its extensive wine and champagne list.

The Gecko Grille is one of our favorite dining spots in these islands. Recently we started with Ocean Escargots, tender young conch served in a garlic-herb butter. We've also enjoyed the spicy conch chowder served in a bread bowl as well as the Italian meat and Provolone quesadilla with red onions and homemade tomato salsa. Entrées include such favorites as grouper macadamia (our favorite) encrusted with avocado and macadamia nuts served over pineapple tomato salsa; fire-roasted pork chop presented with a grilled banana and papaya chutney; chicken breast marinated in papaya juice and cooked over an open flame served with a black bean and melon salsa; and grilled tenderloin of beef cradled in a nest of grilled leeks and carrots with a tri-color peppercorn sauce.

GILLEY'S CAFE AT LEEWARD
☎ 649/946-5094
Moderate
Dress code: casual
Reservations: optional

This delightful eatery, located just steps from the marina at Leeward, serves breakfast, lunch and dinner. We dined here on tender cracked conch, fried to perfection; other options include lobster salad, sirloin steak, seafood and broccoli quiche, and more.

This indoor restaurant is simple, with long tables that encircle a central bar.

> ### ◆ NOTE
>
> If you don't have the chance to dine at Gilley's Café at Leeward, you can still grab a taste of local dishes at Gilley's snack bar at the airport departure lounge. ☎ 649/946-4472.

HEY JOSE'S CARIBBEAN CANTINA
Central Square on Leeward Highway
☎ 649/946-4812
Moderate
Dress code: casual
Reservations: optional

This restaurant serves all types of cuisine, including Mexican dishes, pizza and American food.

KIMONO
Beaches Resort and Spa
☎ 649/946-8000
All-Inclusive
Dress code: casually elegant
Reservations: required

Chefs prepare dishes right at your table Teppanyaki-style in this fun eatery. Start with Caribbean-style sushi or sweet and sour chicken wings, but be sure to save room for main dishes. These include such tempting dishes as pepper-sherry shrimp; glazed mahi mahi teriyaki; and sesame chicken breast.

LE JARDIN RESTAURANT
Le Deck Hotel And Beach Club
Grace Bay
☎ 649/946-5547
Moderate
Dress code: casual
Reservations: optional

Le Jardin offers French and European cuisine, as well as local favorites such as blackened grouper, fish and chips and cracked conch. This beachside restaurant features live music and often draws a late-night crowd on Thursdays and Sundays (also the day for the weekly buffet).

LONE STAR BAR AND GRILL
Ports of Call
☎ 649/946-5832
Inexpensive to Moderate
Dress Code: casual
Reservations: not required

You'll find locals & travelers alike in the lively Lone Star.

Located at the Ports of Call shopping center, this upstairs restaurant specializes in Tex-Mex fare served in a casual bar atmosphere. Live music on Friday nights brings in a crowd.

MARCO POLO'S RESTAURANT
Ports of Call
☎ 649/946-5129
Moderate
Dress code: casual
Reservations: not required

This second-floor restaurant located in the Ports of Call shopping center serves Italian dishes on "Marco Polo's Great Voyage" menu. Enjoy fettucine alfredo, spaghetti with meatballs or veal parmigiana.

We visited here on a Friday night and found the atmosphere lively and fun, with many people enjoying dinner in the small diner and then stepping out on the balcony to listen to live music next door.

SAPODILLA'S
Beaches Resort and Spa
☎ 649/946-8000
All-Inclusive
Dress code: dressy
Reservations: required

International cuisine served in a luxurious atmosphere brings diners to this eatery. Specialties include Canâpés Beaches, a puff pastry shell stuffed with mushrooms, apples, onions and bacon splashed with curry cream sauce; filet of red snapper; filet mignon; blackened pork tenderloin; and sweetened duckling.

SCHOONER'S
Beaches Resort and Spa
☎ 649/946-8000
All-Inclusive
Dress code: dressy
Reservations: required

This specialty restaurant offers local and imported seafood dishes cooked with gourmet flair. Appetizers include steamed mussels in white wine sauce and conch salad. Your main course might be grilled snapper with peppercorn sauce; pan-fried salmon; Alaskan king crab legs; surf and turf; or grilled lobster tails.

SHARKBITE BAR AND GRILL
Admiral's Club at Turtle Cove
☎ 649-941-5090
Moderate
Dress code: casual
Reservations: not required

Sharkbite is Provo's only sports bar.

This waterfront eatery serves lunch and dinner daily. It offers a nightly happy hour with free food. The menu lists American and local offerings, including fish and chips.

SUNSET BAR AND GRILL
Erebus Inn
☎ 649/941-5445 or 946-4240
Moderate
Dress: casually elegant
Reservations: suggested

Fine dining with a French flair is the specialty at this indoor and outdoor restaurant. Open for breakfast, lunch and dinner.

We like the Sunset Bar and Grill for its casual elegance. During our visit, many of the employees were Haitian and spoke in their native language, which gave the bar a nice atmosphere.

THE TERRACE RESTAURANT
Turtle Cove Inn
☎ 649/946-4763
Moderate to Expensive
Dress code: casual
Reservations: suggested

We have fond memories of dining outdoors at this upstairs restaurant. Specialties are conch and local seafood, prepared with a creative twist. Open for lunch and dinner daily except Sunday.

The Terrace Restaurant is a nice place to come after a day spent snorkeling or diving. The atmosphere is relaxed and quiet, aloowing for lots of conversation. Popular with visitors and locals alike.

TIKI HUT
Turtle Cove Inn
☎ 649/941-5341
Inexpensive
Dress code: casual
Reservations: not required

The Tiki Hut offers boxed lunches to go.

This casual restaurant starts the day with Gran Marnier croissant French toast, Belgian waffles and tropical pancakes... and it gets better from there.

We enjoyed an excellent lunch here and sampled the conch fritters, made from the Conch Farm's own product, fish 'n chips and jerk chicken sandwich. Other specialties include pizza, pasta and fish combos and Colorado Black Angus beef.

The restaurant is at the marina and has a fun, boat-loving atmosphere with many locals and expat diners as well as vacationers. There is also an excellent selection of wines from around the world. Open for breakfast, lunch and dinner daily.

Providenciales

Sunup to Sundown

Island Sightseeing

CONCH FARM
☎ 649/946-5849
Hours: 9-4, Monday-Saturday
Admission charged

This is the only farm in the world that raises Queen conch, the shellfish that's become a favorite meal throughout much of the Caribbean. On a guided tour, you'll see conch in various stages, from the larvae in the hatchery to juveniles about 4 mm in length, to adulthood. The operation has three million conch in inventory. There's also a gift shop.

★ DID YOU KNOW?

The product of this unique farm is served at restaurants in Provo, including the Gecko Grille, Anacaona Restaurant and the Tiki Hut.

LITTLE WATER CAY
Admission: free

Save a day to cruise over to Little Water Cay, an island inhabited by friendly iguanas and tropical birds.

◆ NOTE

Most watersports operators on Provo bring day trippers out to this island just off the east end.

The cay is home to the new **Little Water Cay Nature Trail**, designed so that the 20,000 visitors who come to this small island every year can enjoy but not disturb the 1,500 to 2,000 endangered West Indian rock iguanas. Boardwalks have been constructed to allow visitors to see the iguanas and their burrowing systems. You can also climb into observation towers for a view of the cay and the waters.

Golf

Vacationers looking for the opportunity to golf will find it at the 18-hole championship **Provo Golf Club** (☎ 649-946-5991, fax 649-946-5992), frequently cited as one of the top 10 courses in the Caribbean. The club has a pro shop and the Fairways Bar and Grill, which serves breakfast and lunch.

Golfers can hone their skills at a driving range or on putting greens. Eighteen holes, including a shared cart, is $95 ($60 for nine holes); a three-round package is available for $250. Clubs can be rented for $18 for 18 holes or $12 for nine holes.

Golf packages are available from most Provo hotels.

Scuba Diving

Scuba diving and snorkeling are the top attractions of these islands. Visibility ranges from 80 to 100 feet or better and water temperatures hover between 75° and 82° all year long. Divers will see hawksbill turtles, nurse sharks, octopi, colorful fish and more.

A veritable diver's paradise, Provo also has a one-mile long vertical coral wall located offshore.

The Turks and Caicos have established an extensive national park and nature reserve system, with over 31 national parks. These include **Princess Alexandra National Park**, with 13 miles of protected beaches, the **NW Point Marine**, which has spectacular wall diving, and **Chalk Sound**, which offers small boat sailing on the west end of the island.

Providenciales

National Park Rules

While in a national park, be sure to observe the following rules:

- ◎ It is illegal to hunt or fish.

- ◎ It is illegal to remove any animal or coral.

- ◎ Boaters must not moor vessels over 60 feet, except on fixed buoys, or drive boats within 100 yards of the shoreline.

Some good shallow sites are found off Grace Bay. Wreck divers also find challenges here, including the 1985 wreck of the freighter *Southwind*.

You'll find top dive operators on the island to help plan your diving excursions around Provo as well as to other islands in the Turks and Caicos:

ART PICKERING'S PROVO TURTLE DIVERS
Turtle Cove Marina
☎ 649/946-4232

CAICOS ADVENTURES
Banana Cabana at Turtle Cove Marina
☎ 649/941-3346

FLAMINGO DIVERS
Turtle Cove Landing
☎ 649/946-4193

LE DECK DIVING CENTRE
Le Deck Hotel, Grace Bay
☎ 649/946-5547

OCEAN OUTBACK
Grace Bay
☎ 649/941-5810 or 946-4393

SEA DANCER
Caicos Marina & Shipyard
☎ 305/669-9391

SILVER DEEP - PROVO WALL DIVERS
Blue Hills
☎ 649/941-5595

TURKS & CAICOS AGGRESSOR
Liveaboard Dive Boat
☎ 504/385-2416

TURTLE INN DIVERS
Turtle Cove Inn, Turtle Cove
☎ 649/942-3346

Fishing

A couple of fishing companies offer charters around Provo.

DEEP-SEA FISHING CHARTERS
Turtle Cove
☎ 649/946-4394

J&B TOURS
Leeward Marina
☎ 649/946-5047

Shop Till You Drop

Shopping in Provo has improved over the past few years, but is still very limited. Don't expect to see the boutiques of Nassau on this island.

Several small shopping areas offer a selection of gift items, liquors and travel necessities.

Providenciales

The Best Shops

PORTS OF CALL
Grace Bay

Located directly across from the Allegro Resort, this two-story open-air shopping village is home to some of the island's best shops as well as several small restaurants.

Fine Jewelry

ROYAL JEWELS
Arch Plaza, Leeward Highway
☎ 649/946-4699

This shop sells duty-free goods, from 18k jewelry to watches (Tag Heuer, Cartier, Omega), perfumes, crystal, and more.

Watches

GOLD SMITH
Central Square
☎ 649/946-4100

Watches, jewelry, perfumes, cigars and much more are sold here.

Fashion Boutiques

TATTOOED PARROT
Ports of Call, Grace Bay
☎ 649/946-5829

The boutique offers sundresses, shirts, skirts and other clothing.

NIGHT & DAY BOUTIQUE
Ports of Call Village
☎ 649/946-5037

The latest tropical fashions for men and women are available at this shop. Swimwear, shirts, dresses and other clothing items can be purchased here.

Gifts & Souvenirs

GREENSLEEVES
Central Square
☎ 649/946-4147

This shop sells plenty of gifts for your friends back home. Select from among local crafts, art, dolls, jewelry and shells.

THE PIRATE'S CHEST
Ports of Call, Grace Bay
☎ 649/946-5069

They sell all types of souvenirs from hats to shell art to t-shirts.

Art Galleries

BAMBOO GALLERY
Market Place
☎ 649/946-4748

Local and Haitian art are displayed here, with a different artist featured each month. Paintings, sculptures and carvings are for sale.

MAISON CREOLE
Next to Ports of Call, Grace Bay
☎ 649/946-0878

This shop sells all types of Caribbean artwork, from Haitian paintings to small tin accessories painted like Caribbean cottages and small handmade baskets.

Providenciales

After Dark

Nightlife on Provo is fairly quiet. The island has a laid-back atmosphere. Also, the many scuba divers that come here are ready to hit the sack early after a day in the sun and sea, preparing for another day underwater.

However, you'll find live music every night of the week at the island's only casino, found at the Allegro Resort at Grace Bay, where you can try your luck at slots or table games. From there, look to these night-spots for live music on some nights:

EREBUS INN
Turtle Cove
☎ 649/946-4240

Live music and dancing some nights; call for days and times. During our recent visit, Erebus was packed with local residents as well as travelers. The club provides island sounds in a casual atmosphere.

CLUB MED-TURKOISE
Grace Bay
☎ 649/946-5500

We recently bought a night pass at this all-inclusive; you buy tickets for drinks. They have dancing and an evening show. Especially popular with singles.

LE JARDIN RESTAURANT
Le Deck Hotel and Beach Club
Grace Bay
☎ 649/946-5547

Live music entertains diners at Le Jardin, and a late-night crowd is common on Thursdays and Sundays. The atmosphere is fun, with plenty of anglers and divers sharing tales and telling jokes.

LONE STAR BAR AND GRILL
Ports of Call
☎ 649/946-5832

Live music on Friday nights brings in a crowd that includes visitors and locals.

BEACHES RESORT AND SPA
Grace Bay
☎ 649/946-8000

You can buy a night pass at this all-inclusive resort to enjoy their evening show, which varies from live music to island shows. The resort has a family-friendly atmosphere and the shows are suitable for all ages.

Providenciales A-Z

Banks

Bank of Nova Scotia
Town Center Mall
☎ 649/946-4750

First National Bank
Arch Plaza
☎ 649/946-4060

Dentist

Dental Service Ltd.
Leeward Highway
☎ 649/946-4321

Providenciales

Grocery Stores

Payless Provisions
Central Square, Leeward Highway

This shop sells groceries, snacks, water, toiletries, baby supplies and other items you might need. A good place to stock up if you're staying at a property that offers kitchen facilities.

Island Pride Supermarket
Town Center Mall
☎ 649/946-4211

This shop sells everything from grocery items to baked goods and deli foods to health and beauty products.

Emergency Phone Numbers

Dial 911 in case of an emergency.

Health Services/Clinics

MBS Group Medical Practices
Leeward Highway
☎ 649/946-4242

Menzies Medical Practice
Leeward Highway
☎ 649/941-5842

Pharmacies

Island Pharmacy
The Medical Building
Leeward Highway
☎ 649/946-4150

Provo Discount
Leeward Highway
☎ 649/946-4844

Sunset Pharmacy
Central Square, Leeward Highway
☎ 349/941-3751

Grand Turk

Grand Turk is home of its own little historic controversy. We said earlier in the book that many historians believe Columbus first made landfall in the New World on the Bahamian island of San Salvador. However, many others believe that the island the Italian explorer called "Guanahani" wasn't the Bahamian island, but instead was Grand Turk.

The truth about where Columbus first set foot on land may never be known, but many facts are proven about Grand Turk's often raucous history. The island was settled by pirates from Bermuda. These devilish entrepreneurs used the nearby coral reefs as their own traps, luring ships in with lights to a false sense of safety. When the ships wrecked on the coral reefs, out went the pirates to plunder them. Today the evidence of that wicked history is still evident on Grand Turk; many of the historic buildings were made from the lumber of these ships.

The atmosphere is quiet and calm on Grand Turk. This island serves as the governmental capital of the Turks and Caicos Islands and you'll see many government buildings in the community of Cockburn Town. Here most of the island's 4,300 residents live just steps from the sea.

Best Places to Stay

ARAWAK INN AND BEACH CLUB
White Sands Beach, southwest side of Grand Turk
☎ 649/946-2277, fax 649/946-2279
Reservations: ☎ 888/880-4477
Moderate
E-mail: reservations@arawakinn.com

This hotel located south of Governor's Beach offers 15 units with diving and horseback riding available. Rooms have cable TV and air-conditioning. Facilities include a freshwater pool, restaurant and beach bar.

CORAL REEF CONDOMINIUM AND BEACH CLUB
The Ridge
☎ 649/946-2055, fax 649/946-2911
Reservations: ☎ 800/418-4704
E-mail: gthotels@tciway.tc
Inexpensive

Located on the island's windward side, Coral Reef provides 18 studio and one-bedroom apartment units with kitchen facilities, air-conditioning, balconies, telephones and cable TV. Guests have access to the freshwater swimming pool, Jacuzzi, tennis courts, fitness center and meeting facilities. This casual resort is a good place to kick back and enjoy the peacefulness of Grand Turk.

SALT RAKER INN
Duke Street
☎ 649/946-2260, fax 649/946-2817
E-mail sraker@tciway.tc
www.microplan.com/~paradise
Inexpensive

This small property offers 10 guest rooms and three suites, each with air conditioning, cable TV and ceiling fans. The inn is home to a restaurant and is within walking distance from the beach.

SITTING PRETTY HOTEL
Cockburn Town
☎ 649/946-2232, fax 649/946-2668
Reservations: ☎ 800/418-4704
Inexpensive to Moderate

Sitting Pretty was formerly Hotel Kittina.

The hotel includes a 5-star PADI dive shop, along with 24 air-conditioned guest rooms. Some hotel rooms are right on the beach in Cockburn Town; others are across the street. The hotel has a pool, restaurant and bar.

TURKS HEAD INN
Duke Street
☎ 649/946-2466, fax 649/0946-2825
Inexpensive to Moderate

This circa 1860 mansion was once a governor's private guest house and now offers antique-filled air-conditioned guest rooms, a restaurant, bar and live entertainment some evenings.

Grand Turk

Best Places to Eat

ARAWAK INN RESTAURANT AND BAR
White Sands Beach
☎ 649/946-2277 or 2276
Inexpensive
Dress code: casual
Reservations: not required

You can enjoy Bahamian as well as American dishes at this casual eatery. Local seafood is the specialty of the house, and on Saturday nights there's a barbecue. You can dine indoors or outside with a view of the sea. Open for breakfast, lunch and dinner.

SECRET GARDEN
Salt Raker Inn, Duke Street
☎ 649/946-2260
Inexpensive
Dress code: casual
Reservations: not required

The restaurant is open for breakfast, lunch and dinner and features local cuisine as well as American dishes. On Wednesday and Sunday nights the restaurant hosts a barbecue and sing-along.

TURKS HEAD INN
Duke Street
☎ 649/946-2466
Inexpensive
Dress code: casually elegant
Reservations: not required

This casual eatery serves up breakfast, lunch and dinner. Start the evening in the pub or stop by for an after-dinner drink and local music. Caribbean cuisine is the house specialty, although you'll also find International cuisine. A selection of wines is offered.

THE WATER'S EDGE
Duke Street
☎ 649/946-1680
Inexpensive
Dress code: casual
Reservations: not required

This bistro serves local seafood in a fun and relaxing setting on the beach. Open for lunch and dinner nightly.

Sunup to Sundown

Island Sightseeing

TURKS AND CAICOS NATIONAL MUSEUM
Main Street, Cockburn Town
☎ 649/946-2160
Hours: Monday-Friday, 10-4; Saturday, 10-1
Admission charged

It may have been, as the story always goes, a dark and stormy night that caused the Molasses Reef shipwreck nearly 500 years ago. Or the weather may have been perfectly clear, the ship lured onto the coral by buccaneers on the shore falsely signaling safe passage.

Whatever the reason, the Spanish caravel hit the reef, sinking quickly in only 20 feet of water. There it remained, encased in a heavy coat of sediment and barnacles, until the 1970s. When the wreck was excavated, it proved to be the oldest European shipwreck in the New World.

Today, artifacts from the wreck are on display in the Turks and Caicos National Museum, itself a buried treasure. The National Museum, with its interactive displays, video presentations and scientific exhibits, would be a special attraction in any city with a rich maritime history. It is especially surprising, however, to find it on an island only seven miles square with a population of just 3,700.

The museum is located in the former Guinip House, one of the oldest buildings on Grand Turk. This 150-year-old home was built in the colonial style used by the Bermudans who settled this island. Like many other Grand Turk buildings, the house was constructed from the lumber of wooden ships.

Historical Bluff

The attention of the world was focused on the Turks and Caicos during the excavation of this wreck when the initial salvagers tried to claim that this was Columbus' *Pinta*. In reality, the ship was not a part of Columbus' fleet, but one whose purpose was probably illegal. "We don't know the name of this ship," explains curator Brian M. Riggs, "but we know why we don't know."

Like drug-running planes of today, ships transporting illegal booty were purposely kept off the official records of Spain. Three pair of two-person leg irons, recovered in a locked position, and rare Lucayan pottery indicate that the ship was probably en route with illegal slaves bound for the plantations of Hispaniola.

When it was discovered that the salvagers were trying to obtain funding by claiming this was the *Pinta,* the government of the Turks and Caicos reclaimed the wreck and turned it over to the Texas A&M-based Ships of Discovery, a nonprofit archaeological research group. The group took over the laborious task of removing items and carefully cataloging each piece, then trying to undo the years of damage the sea had wrought.

Many artifacts can be seen in this museum. Three downstairs rooms are dedicated to shipwrecks, with one room covering the Molasses Reef site, another the archaeology and scientific processes involved in an excavation, and the third filled with artifacts. Other exhibits explain more about the structure of Age of Discovery caravel ships and the history of the Turks and Caicos.

Scuba Diving

The waters here are a favorite with scuba divers. Grand Turk has miles of drop-off diving surrounding its shores. Night dives are especially popular, when the colors of the reefs take on a phosphorescent glow.

In Grand Turk, check with **Blue Water Divers**, ☎ 649/946-2432; **Sea Eye Diving,** ☎ 649/946-1407; and **Aquanaut**, ☎ 649/946-2160.

Banks

Bank of Nova Scotia
Town Centre Mall, Grand Turk
☎ 649/946-2506

Turks and Caicos Banking Company
Duke Street
☎ 649/946-2364

North Caicos

*T*hey call it the "garden island," and a quick look around North Caicos explains why. This island receives twice as much rain as Providenciales and most other destinations in the Turks and Caicos. The rainfall helps North Caicos produce sea grapes, sugar apples, oranges, mangoes and other tropical harvests.

Flamingos can also be seen at the Mud Hold Pond.

This island is home to the ruins of several Loyalist plantations. Another interesting site is the Flamingo Pond, where magnificent flamingos nest.

◆ **TIP**

Birders should make time to visit nearby Three Mary's Cay for a look at ospreys.

Best Places to Stay

PELICAN BEACH HOTEL
Whitby
☎ 649/946-7112, fax 649/946-7139
Moderate to Expensive

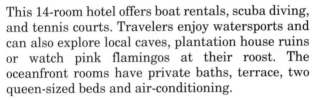

This 14-room hotel offers boat rentals, scuba diving, and tennis courts. Travelers enjoy watersports and can also explore local caves, plantation house ruins or watch pink flamingos at their roost. The oceanfront rooms have private baths, terrace, two queen-sized beds and air-conditioning.

PROSPECT OF WHITBY HOTEL
Whitby
☎ 649/946-7119, fax 649/946-7114
Inexpensive to Moderate

This relaxed oceanfront resort offers 28 guest rooms along with tennis courts, dive shop, watersports and fishing. It is ideal for those looking to get away from it all with few distractions. Bury your cell phone in the sand and enjoy a few days without radios, TVs or newspapers. Rooms have air-conditioning and a ceiling fan. The hotel also has a restaurant.

Best Places to Eat

OCEAN BEACH HOTEL RESTAURANT
Whitby
☎ 649/946-7113
Moderate
Dress code: casual, casually elegant
Reservations: required

This restaurant, located at Ocean Beach Condominiums, serves lunch and dinner by reservation only. Dine on Caribbean or International dishes.

The Oceanfront Beach Hotel Restaurant is popular with locals & visitors.

North Caicos

PROSPECT OF WHITBY HOTEL RESTAURANT
Whitby
☎ 649/946-7119
Moderate
Dress code: casually elegant
Reservations: recommended

Dine on Italian cuisine at this restaurant that is open for breakfast, lunch and dinner.

PELICAN BEACH HOTEL RESTAURANT
Whitby
☎ 649/946-7112
Moderate
Dress code: casual
Reservations: suggested

Dine indoors or out at this hotel restaurant that features local and American dishes. Located on the north shore, this casual restaurant is a good place to unwind after a day on the beach. Don't miss the homemade breads and desserts!

Menu selections include Caribbean lobster, conch, ribs and chicken.

North Caicos A-Z

Grocery Stores

Al's Food Store of North Caicos
Bottle Creek
☎ 649/946-7248

Middle Caicos

This middle child of the island trio is no shy violet; Middle Caicos is larger than its nearby sister islands and sometimes even termed "Grand Caicos." Fifteen miles long and 13 miles wide, the island is largely undeveloped and is home to just about 300 residents.

The island has a rich history. It was once home to the Taino Indians around 750 AD.

★ DID YOU KNOW?

The Taino Indians were later renamed the Lucayans when explorers reached the island on the feast of St. Luke's Day.

At one time, about 4,000 Tainos lived on the island and their artifacts are still being discovered on the island's sandy beaches and in its many limestone caves. One archaeological excavation revealed a ceremonial court that also served as a ball court. Historians believe rubber balls from the Amazon were once used on the court, although we have no explanation as to how the balls arrived from there.

Later the island became a pirate's lair. Pierre Le Grand captured a Spanish treasure ship near the islands around 1640 and for years the island served as a hideout for pirates such as Calico Jack Rackam, Ann Bonny and Mary Reade.

One aspect of the island that may have attracted those pirates were its many caves. Caves over

120,000 years old are the most dramatic above-water caverns in the Caribbean. The **Conch Bar Caves** were a sacred site to the Tainos. Part of the caverns have never been explored and local guides can take travelers to view the giant stalagmite and stalactite formations, underground lakes and more. The caves are inhabited by four bat species and giant white owls with a wingspan of five feet.

Best Place to Stay

BLUE HORIZON RESORT
One mile northeast of the airport,
along Crossing Place Trail
☎ 649/946-6141, fax 649/946-6139
Moderate
www.bhresort.com

This small resort offers rental cottages that include full kitchen and daily maid service. Accommodations include Sunset Cottage for two people (with daily maid service) and Whale Watch, a two-bedroom, two-bathroom home for four or five guests (maid service extra).

During high season (December through February), the property opens a restaurant.

Sunup to Sundown

Island Sights

You might want to consider a taxi tour around Middle Caicos. One of the highlights is **Mugjin Harbour**, which has a beautiful beach.

The island also boasts an extensive **cave system** at Conch Bar, with stalactites and stalagmites. Talk with your hotel staff about hiring a guide if you are not an experienced caver.

Middle Caicos also has several **archeological sites**. Excavation is most developed at Armstrong Pond, where a Lucayan ball court has been uncovered.

Birders should head to **Northwest Point**. Here, mangrove swamps harbor many bird species.

Scuba Diving

Dive boats come from nearby islands to bring scuba buffs to these clear waters. Reefs and wall dives are the big attraction. A favorite dive spot just off the shores of Middle Caicos is the **Blue Hole**. Easily visible from the air, this round depression in the reef is hundreds of feet deep and requires the skills of advanced divers. Sharks, rays, groupers and sea turtles frequent the navy blue waters of this underwater sinkhole. Many of Provo's dive operators offer excursions out to Middle Caicos.

ART PICKERING'S PROVO TURTLE DIVERS
Turtle Cove Marina
☎ 649/946-4232

CAICOS ADVENTURES
Banana Cabana at Turtle Cove Marina
☎ 649/941-3346

FLAMINGO DIVERS
Turtle Cove Landing
☎ 649/946-4193

LE DECK DIVING CENTRE
Le Deck Hotel, Grace Bay
☎ 649/946-5547

OCEAN OUTBACK
Grace Bay
☎ 649/941-5810 or 946-4393

SEA DANCER
Caicos Marina & Shipyard
☎ 305/669-9391

SILVER DEEP - PROVO WALL DIVERS
Blue Hills
☎ 649/941-5595

TURKS & CAICOS AGGRESSOR
Liveaboard Dive Boat
☎ 504/385-2416

TURTLE INN DIVERS
Turtle Cove Inn, Turtle Cove
☎ 649/942-3346

Sportfishing

Sportfishing boats come from nearby islands to try their luck in these rich waters.

DEEP-SEA FISHING CHARTERS
Turtle Cove
☎ 649/946-4394

J&B TOURS
Leeward Marina
☎ 649/946-5047

Pine Cay

Pine Cay is for those who really want to get away from it all. Privately owned, the 800-acre island is dotted with willowy casuarina trees, pretty beaches and a single resort.

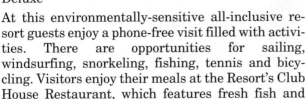

Best Place to Stay & Eat

THE MERIDIAN CLUB
Pine Cay
Reservations: ☎ 800/331-9154
fax 649/946-5128
Deluxe

At this environmentally-sensitive all-inclusive resort guests enjoy a phone-free visit filled with activities. There are opportunities for sailing, windsurfing, snorkeling, fishing, tennis and bicycling. Visitors enjoy their meals at the Resort's Club House Restaurant, which features fresh fish and healthy dishes prepared by an award-winning chef.

Salt Cay

Tiny Salt Cay is the kind of place you come to for real rest and relaxation. There are very few diversions on this small cay – just some fields that were once flooded with seawater, later to evaporate and be raked of sea salt. In those days, this 2½-square-mile landmass was the world's largest producer of salt. Remnants of old windmills still turn in the gentle trade winds, a reminder of that bygone era.

Today Salt Cay is the kind of place where you can pedal around on a bike and not worry about traffic. Beautiful waters surround the cay, inviting snorkelers and scuba divers.

Best Places to Stay

MOUNT PLEASANT GUEST HOUSE
Victoria Street
Reservations: ☎ 888/332-3133, 649/946-6927
Inexpensive

This simple accommodation with seven guest rooms plus a dorm room with multiple beds is a favorite with scuba divers. All rooms are furnished with antiques and, while they're nothing fancy, they are within walking distance of the beach. A casual restaurant located on the property is a super place to meet fellow travelers.

WINDMILLS PLANTATION
North Beach Road
☎ 649/946-6962, fax 649/946-6930
Reservations: ☎ 800/822-7715
Expensive
E-mail: plantation@tciway.tc

It's somewhat surprising to find this exclusive eight-room hotel tucked away on tiny Salt Cay. Perhaps that's what makes this inn so special. It features furniture imported from Costa Rica, a library with over a thousand volumes, a restaurant featuring Caribbean food, including Salt Cay lobster, and horseback and nature trails. It's a romantic getaway offering the ultimate in privacy.

The most lavish property on Salt Cay and one of the most exquisite in the entire region, this all-inclusive offers eight rooms and four suites, two with private plunge pools.

Best Places to Eat

MT. PLEASANT GUEST HOUSE
Victoria Street
☎ 649/946-6927
Inexpensive
Dress code: casual
Reservations: not required

We have fond memories of an excellent lunch at this casual eatery. We had flown to Salt Cay for the day, ate at this garden restaurant behind the bed and breakfast, and then enjoyed a walk around town as our pilot napped in a hammock in the garden: true island relaxation.

THE WINDMILLS
North Beach Road
☎ 649/946-6962
Expensive
Dress code: casually elegant or dressy
Reservations: required

Try Salt Cay lobster and other local dishes served with a gourmet flair at this elegant eatery.

Salt Cay

Sunup to Sundown

Island Sightseeing

WHALE WATCHING
Admission charged
Hours: December through April only

Nature lovers find plenty of activity on this tiny isle. From December though April, humpback whales can be spotted in the Turks Islands Passage between Salt Cay and Grand Turk.

Scuba Diving

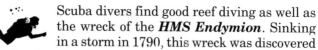

Scuba divers find good reef diving as well as the wreck of the *HMS Endymion*. Sinking in a storm in 1790, this wreck was discovered by dive operator and Mount Pleasant innkeeper Brian Sheedy. While much of the wreck has been lost to time, the massive cannons still rest on the ocean's floor along with four giant anchors.

For scuba diving while on Salt Cay, call **Porpoise Divers**, ☎ 649/946-6927.

South Caicos

Outh Caicos is not an island you want to go if you enjoy an abundance of activities. There's not much to keep you entertained here – you simply have to entertain yourself or just enjoy the peace and quiet of this island that's the home of much of the Turks and Caicos' fishing industry.

Most activity here takes place in **Cockburn Harbour**, from which conch and spiny lobster are exported. Have a look at the bustling harbor, then hire a taxi driver for an impromptu tour of the island. One popular stop is the "boiling hole," a natural blowhole where the sea is forced through gaps in the stone, spraying water and mist in the air. This is a good stop when there is a lot of wave action.

Don't forget to bring your camera to the boiling hole.

Best Places to Stay

SOUTH CAICOS OCEAN HAVEN
East Bay
☎ 649/946-3444
Inexpensive to Moderate
www.southcaicosoceanhaven.com

This small facility now operates as a self-catered timeshare. Just five minutes from the property you'll find excellent diving and the opportunity to see reef sharks, barracuda, turtles, morays and more. The vast majority of guests here are divers who spend most of the day diving, getting ready to dive or talking about their last dive!

South Caicos

Sunup to Sundown

Island Sightseeing

It's worth making a brief island tour. One site of interest is the **Boiling Hole**. Water from here filled the salt pans from which salt was harvested.

Scuba Diving

Guided dives and equipment are available through **South Caicos Ocean Haven,** ☎ 649/946-3444.

Island Cuisine

Tastes of the Islands

It's time for your taste buds to enjoy a holiday as well. You've found a good destination – on a visit to the Bahamas you'll encounter traditional Bahamian food and, especially on the larger islands such as New Providence and Grand Bahama, a sampling of cuisines from around the globe.

Popular Foods

Just what is Bahamian cuisine? These dishes feature fresh local seafood and plenty of spices.

Conch is pronounced KonK.

One of the main ingredients found on a Bahamian menu is **conch**. You're probably familiar with this mollusk because of its shell: a beautiful pink curl that can measure nearly a foot long. When blown by those in the know, it can become an island bullhorn. The conch are caught in the sea (and, in the Turks and Caicos, also farmed like catfish or crawfish). The shell covers a huge piece of white meat with an almost rubbery texture, as well as a "foot," the appendage used by the conch to drag itself along the ocean floor in search of food. Conch makes its way to the Bahamian menu in many forms – chopped, sliced, diced, fried, marinated – and is served just about every imaginable way.

To tenderize the conch, the meat is scored with a knife, soaked in lime juice and spices, and sometimes even pounded.

The ways of cooking conch are numerous: cracked, in salad, as chowder or fritters & more!

Another Bahamian favorite is the **rock lobster,** a clawless lobster that is served many ways. **Crab** is also found on many menus, along with the ubiquitous **grouper** and **snapper**.

Turks and Caicos, with its arid climate, is not like the breadbasket tropical islands of Jamaica or St. Lucia fame. Little is grown here; most must be imported and grocery prices attest to that.

However, you will find a few items grown locally. North Caicos produces **sea grapes, sugar apples, mangoes** and **sapodillas.** Also, the surrounding seas are rich in **seafood**, including grouper, tuna, hogfish and shellfish, especially conch and spiny lobster. You'll also see **turtle**, **dolphin** (the fish, not the mammal), and **goat** on some area menus. A hydroponic farm on Provo supplies some vegetables.

You'll find a wide selection of food in these islands, reflecting the popular tourism industry as well as the many expats who make the Turks and Caicos their home.

Cooking for Yourself

If you are staying in a condo or accommodation with kitchen facilities, you may even want to purchase your own seafood and cook it up Bahamian style.

Do as the locals do and buy it right on the waterfront. In Nassau, seafood vendors can be found at:

- ◎ **Potter's Cay**, right at the base of the Paradise Island Bridge

- 🌀 **Eastern Road** on Montagu Beach
- 🌀 **Arawak Cay** on West Bay Street
- 🌀 **Paradise Island dock**

Prices are subject to good-natured haggling and some vendors also sell cooked (often fried) seafood as well. Many stalls will prepare the conch for you in a matter of minutes, dicing and spicing the raw conch with a marinade of peppers and onions. Along with conch, stalls also sell grouper, bonefish, snapper, crawfish and Bahamian lobster in season.

Real Taste of the Bahamas

If your goal is to search out real Bahamian cuisine, your task is now much easier thanks to the "Real Taste of the Bahamas" program. A cooperative effort of the Ministry of Tourism, the Ministry of Agriculture and Fisheries, and the Restaurant Association of the Bahamas, this program seeks to promote independent restaurants that offer a quality dining experience while utilizing and showcasing indigenous food products.

To join the program, restaurants must:

- 🌀 use Bahamian produce, fresh fish, meats, dairy produce whenever possible and have fresh fruits and vegetables in season
- 🌀 provide the highest standards of cleanliness in the dining rooms and kitchen
- 🌀 have at least one person on staff trained and knowledgeable about the Bahamas, a BahamaHost graduate

Island Cuisine

⊚ treat guests with every possible courtesy and provide the best possible service to patrons

Identifying member restaurants is easy, thanks to the Real Taste of the Bahamas logo displayed by qualifying eateries. The banner, highlighted by a conch and pineapple, identifies member restaurants.

For more on the program, contact the **Real Taste of the Bahamas**, PO Box N-3701, Nassau, New Providence, Bahamas or ☎ 242/322-7500, ext. 2086.

Participating restaurants include:

Androsia, West Bay Street, Cable Beach, New Providence Island, ☎ 242/327-7805.

Anthony's Caribbean Grill, East Casino Drive, Paradise Island, ☎ 242/363-3152.

Avery's, Adelaide Village, New Providence Island, ☎ 242/326-1547.

Bahamian Kitchen, Trinity Place, New Providence Island, ☎ 242/325-0702.

Buena Vista, Deveaux Street off Bay Street, Nassau, New Providence Island, ☎ 242/322-2811.

Café Johnny Canoe, West Bay Street, Cable Beach, New Providence Island, ☎ 242/327-3373.

Capriccio, West Bay Street, Cable Beach, New Providence Island, ☎ 242/327-8547.

Comfort Zone, #5 Wulff Road, Nassau, New Providence Island, ☎ 242/323-2676.

Conch Fritters Bar and Grill, Marlborough Street, Nassau, New Providence Island, ☎ 242/323-8801.

Anthony's Caribbean Grill, East Casino Drive, Paradise Island, ☎ 242/363-3152.

Europe, West Bay Street, Nassau, New Providence Island, ☎ 242/322-8032.

Junkanoo Café, Colony Place Arcade, Bay Street, Nassau, New Providence Island, ☎ 242/328-7944.

Mama Lyddy's Place, Market Street, Nassau, New Providence Island, ☎ 242/328-6849.

Montagu Gardens Steak and Grill, East Bay Street, Nassau, New Providence Island, ☎ 242/394-6347.

The Poop Deck, East Bay Street, Nassau, New Providence Island, ☎ 242/393-8175.

Sun And..., Lakeview Road off Shirley Street, Nassau, New Providence Island, ☎ 242/393-2644.

Tony Roma's, West Bay Street, Nassau, New Providence Island, ☎ 242/325-2020.

Travellers Rest, West Bay Street, Nassau, New Providence Island, ☎ 242/327-7633.

Drinks of the Islands

Recently beer and a rum began to be produced in the Turks and Caicos. **Caya,** both Pilsner and Pale Ale, is available in bottles and draft. These brews are bottled by the Turks and Caicos Brewing Company.

The local rum, made from sugarcane grown on other islands, is **Lucayan**. This dark rum is distilled by the Lucayan Rum Company Limited.

In the Bahamas, residents and visitors will find plenty of liquid refreshment, both alcoholic and non-alcoholic. The islands are home to **Kalik beer**,

Island Cuisine

an amber-colored drink that cools travelers on hot days.

Among locals, the top drink is **gin and coconut water**. (Don't use coconut milk, which is much heavier.) Some sweeten the mix by adding condensed milk and pieces of jelly coconut.

Spices of the Bahamas

The spices grown on the Bahamas give the regional cuisine its distinctive flavors. If you plan to cook for yourself, you should experiment with some of the following spices:

Annatto. This spice, a derivative of a shrub, is used like saffron in soups, stews and other dishes. It gives food a red color.

Curry. This combination of many spices (turmeric, cardamom, cumin, cinnamon, mace and others) flavors many island dishes.

Scallion. This member of the onion family frequently appears in Bahamian recipes.

Nutmeg. Order a rum punch in most island bars and you'll have a look at a popular use of nutmeg: sprinkled on top of the potent drink. Nutmeg is a popular spice here. The tree grows naturally throughout the island and produces a seed, called the nutmeg. A red, stringy covering around the seed is called mace.

Vanilla. The vanilla bean comes from the vanilla plant, an orchid. It is used in a variety of foods and drinks, including tropical cocktails and desserts.

Menu Items

If you are a hesitant eater, have no fear: you will find "traditional" American breakfasts and other meals served at every resort on the island.

However, when you're ready to give your taste buds a holiday as well, look to local dishes for a pick-me-up. Here are some of the most popular island dishes that you'll see frequently on restaurant menus.

Benne seed cake. These sesame seed cakes (called benne seeds in Africa) are a favorite snack.

Chicken souse. This Bahamian soup (pronounced SoWSe) is served throughout the day and made with boiled chicken, chicken giblets, onion, celery, lime, hot peppers and allspice.

Conch fritters. This tasty appetizer is a fried bread with bits of conch and seasonings. It is usually served with a red dipping sauce such as cocktail sauce.

Many swear that conch is an aphrodisiac.

Conch chowder. This tasty soup incorporates local conch fresh from the sea.

Conch salad. Walk along the waterfront in Nassau and you can buy this delicious dish from any number of small stands. The dish is made from conch, tomatoes, onion, celery, hot peppers, lime juice and sour orange. Much like ceviche, the citrus juices cook the sliced conch.

Cracked conch. This deep-fried entrée is a favorite lunch offering.

Fish and grits. Boiled fish and grits are a favorite Bahamian breakfast dish.

Island Cuisine

Fish tea. This spicy soup looks and tastes much better than it sounds. Like a fish bouillon, this broth captures the taste of the sea. Watch out for fish bones!

Grouper. This large fish makes its appearance on just about every restaurant menu. The mild fish may be served broiled, fried and just about every other imaginable way.

Guava duff. The number one Bahamian dessert is made similar to a jelly roll. Peeled and seeded guavas are rolled in a dough that has been boiled and baked. The confection is then covered with a thick sauce made from guava pulp, eggs, sugar, evaporated milk and either brandy or rum.

Johnny cake. Sometimes called journey cakes (since you could carry them along on your journey), these cakes are actually fried or baked breads. They're a favorite accompaniment to saltfish.

In Jamaica this dish is known as rice and peas.

Peas and rice. This dish is found on just about every lunch and dinner plate in the Bahamas.

Saltfish. Dried, salted fish used in all kinds of recipes from soups to entrées. This ingredient is hugely popular in Jamaica, but makes only rare appearances in the Bahamian kitchen.

Souse. Pronounced "SoWSe", this soup is a Bahamian favorite and includes celery, peppers and a meat (usually chicken, oxtail or pig's feet).

Stew fish. This stew is made with fish, celery, onions, tomatoes and plenty of spices.

Turtle soup. This thick soup features local turtle meat, cut into chunks.

Turtle steak. The green turtle makes its appearance on many island menus; the taste is similar to veal.

Ordering Food Items by Mail

Check out these Internet sites and mail order companies to bring home a taste of the islands any time.

Hot Sauces

Gourmet International Distributors, Inc.
☎ 800/273-7252
www.hotsauceetc.com
e-mail: info@hotsauceetc.com

Gourmet International sells Pickappeppa sauce (both brown and red), Walker's Wood jerk sauce and other good brands.

Jamaica Standard Products Company Ltd.
☎ 800/240-6043
www.caribplace.com/foods/jspcl.htm
e-mail: sanco@colis.com

Baronhall Farms' products include Hell Hot Pepper Concentrate, Scotch Bonnet Pepper Sauce and Jamaican Hot Curry Sauce. They are sold through Jamaica Standard Products Company.

Spices

World Harbors
www.maine.com/worldharbors/
This site offers sauces and marinades.

Island Cuisine

General Information Sources

Internet Sites

The Bahamas

www.grand-bahama.com
The official web page of the Grand Bahama Island Tourism Board, this site includes information on where to stay, what to do and nature. It features a newsgroup where you can get travelers' tips.

www.thebahamas.com
This is the Bahamas online, where you can pick up information on island facts, hotels, shopping and dining. It features a travel guide to Nassau, Bimini and Abaco.

www.bahamas.com
Official website of the Islands of the Bahamas. Information on the history of the islands, how to get there, the people of the Bahamas, where to stay, travel tips, tourist offices, doing business in the Bahamas and more.

www.bahamasweb.com
This site includes a tourist guide, restaurant guide, hotel information, weather and more.

Out Islands

The following websites offer more specific information about smaller islands or are run by island resorts and hotels.

Abaco

Abaco Beach Resort
www.greatabacobeach.com

Banyan Beach Club
www.banyanbeach.com

Bluff House Beach Hotel
www.oi.net/BluffHouse

Coco Bay Cottages
www.oi.net/cocobay

Different Of Abaco
www.oi.net/different/web

Dolphin Beach Resort
www.dolphinbeachresort.com

Green Turtle Club
www.greenturtleclub.com

Guana Beach Resort and Marina
www.guanabeach.com

Guana Seaside Village
www.guanaseaside.com

Hope Town Harbour Lodge
www.hopetownlodge.com

Hope Town Hideaways
www.hopetown.com

Pelican Beach Villas
www.ivacation.com/p2613.htm

Sea Spray Resort and Marina
www.seasprayresort.com

Treasure Cay Hotel Resort
www.treasurecay.com

Treehouse By the Sea
www.oii.net/treehouse

Turtle Hill Vacation Villas
www.turtlehill.com

Andros

Point of View Villas
www.pointofviewbahamas.com

Seascape Inn
www.seascapeinn.com

Small Hope Bay Lodge
www.smallhope.com

Berry Islands

Chub Cay Club
www.chubcay.com

Bimini

Bimini Big Game Club and Marina
www.bimini-big-game-club.com

Cat Island

Fernandez Bay Village
www.fernandexbayvillage.com

Greenwood Beach Resort
www.hotelgreenwoodinn.com

Hawk's Nest Resort
www.hawks-nest.com

Crooked Island

Pittstown Point Landing
www.pittstown.com

Eleuthera

Cambridge Villas
www.ivacation.com/p421.htm

The Coves Eleuthera
www.thecoveeleuthera.com

Palmetto Shores Villas
www.ivacation.com/p6835.htm

Rainbow Inn
www.rainbowinn.com

Unique Village
www.bahamasvg.com/uniquevil.html

Ventaclub Eleuthera
www.ivv.it

Exuma

Coconut Cove
www.exhumabahamas.com/coconutcove.html

Hotel Higgins Landing
www.higginslanding.com

Peace & Plenty
www.peaceandplenty.com

Regatta Point
www.exumabahamas.com/regattapoint.html

Staniel Cay Yacht Club
www.stanielcay.com

Two Turtles Inn
www.twoturtlesinn.com

Harbour Island

Coral Sands
www.coralsands.com

Dunmore Beach Club
www.dunmorebeach.com

Pink Sands
www.islandoutpost.com

Romora Bay Club
www.romorabay.com

Runaway Hill Club
www.cpscaribnet.com/runaway/runa.htm

Valentine's Resort and Marina
www.valentinesdive.com

Long Island

Cape Santa Maria Resort
www.obmg.com

Stella Maris
www.stellamaris.com

Bibliography

Baker, Christopher P. *Lonely Planet Bahamas, Turks and Caicos*. Lonely Planet, 1998.

Charles, Ron. *Open Road Bahamas Guide*. Open Road Press, 1997.

Cohen, Steve, Janet Groene, Laurie Werner, Ute Vladimir, et al. *Caribbean: The Greater Antilles, Bermuda, Bahamas*. Nelles Verlag, 1997.

Dulles, Wink and Marael Johnson. *Fielding's Bahamas*. Fielding Worldwide, 1996.

Fleming, Carol B. *Adventuring in the Caribbean: The Sierra Club Travel Guide to the 40 Islands of the Caribbean Sea including the Bahamas, Jamaica, and the Dominican Republic*. Sierra Club Books, 1989.

Guttermann, Steve and Philip Z. Trupp. *Diver's Almanac: Guide to the Bahamas and Caribbean*. Triton Publishing, 1987.

Henderson, James S. *The Caribbean and the Bahamas, 4th Edition*. Cadogan, 1997.

Howard, Blair. *Adventure Guide to the Bahamas, 2nd Edition*. Hunter Publishing, 1999.

Huber, Joyce and Jon. *Best Dives of the Bahamas, Bermuda, the Florida Keys and Turks & Caicos.* Hunter Publishing, 2000.

Huber, Joyce and Jon. *Best Diving Adventures in the Bahamas, Bermuda, Caribbean, Hawaii and the Florida Keys.* Photographics Publishing, 1998.

Jeffrey, Nan. *Bahamas: Out Island Odyssey.* Menasha Ridge Press, 1995.

Keller, Bob and Charlotte Keller. *Diving and Snorkeling Guide to the Bahamas Family Islands and Grand Bahama.* Pisces Books, 1994.

McMorran, Jennifer. *Ulysses Travel Guide of the Bahamas.* Ulysses Books, 1998.

Pavlidis, Stephen J. *The Exuma Guide: A Cruising Guide to the Exuma Cays: Approaches, Routes, Anchorages, Dive Sites, Flora, Fauna, and Lore of the Exuma Cays.* Seaworthy Publications, 1997.

Pavlidis, Stephen J. *On and Off the Beaten Path: The Central Southern Bahamas: from South Florida to the Turks and Caicos.* Seaworthy Publications, 1998.

Permenter, P. and Bigley, J. *The Bahamas: A Taste of the Islands.* Hunter Publishing, 2000.

Porter, Darwin. *Frommer's The Bahamas.* Frommer, 1997.

Wilson, Matthew. *The Bahamas Cruising Guide.* McGraw-Hill, 1998.

Information Sources

Index